Dick E. Bird's Birdfeeding 101

MalleryBooks

Richard E. Mallery

a.k.a. Dick E. Bird

MALLERYBOOKS

New York   London   Toronto   Sydney   Acme

Dick E. Bird's Birdfeeding 101

A Tongue-in-Beak Guide to
Suet, Seed, and Squirrelly Neighbors

Published by **MALLERYBOOKS**

Visit our Web site at www.thedickebirdnews.com

For a sample copy of *The Dick E. Bird News*
visit our website:
thedickebirdnews.com

Mallery, Richard E.
    Dick E. Bird's Birdfeeding 101: A Tongue-in-Beak
Guide to Suet, Seed, and Squirrelly Neighbors
—Revised Edition

1. Birds—Feeding and feeds. 2. Birds—Humor.

ISBN 978-0-9796696-0-6

To the hope that bird feeding can illustrate the importance of biodiversity to those who discover the magic of nature perched outside their window.

—Keep Smilin', Dick E. Bird

Contents

Hairy Houdini is a nationally syndicated columnist. His views are his alone and not necessarily those of *The Dick E. Bird News*. Except when he says nice stuff about us!

Introduction

By Hairy Houdini, Squirrel-in-Residence

Birdfeeding is a wonderful way to enjoy nature right outside your window. This book answers every question imaginable on the subject — and then some. It is the only book that accurately describes what can be done to keep us squirrels from eating birdseed: NOTHING!

Birdfeeding would not be as popular today if not for us squirrels. We keep things interesting.

Anyone who has spent time observing birdfeeders in his yard knows there is a very complicated cold war raging. Let me point out that we squirrels did not realize until just recently that all that seed, suet and nectar was not for us. If you think, now that we know, we are going to quit eating it — get real!

Let's say you are very hungry and someone puts you in a room with a smorgasbord and tells you not to eat anything — then leaves you by yourself. The first thing you are going to do is fill your face as soon as you think it's safe.

That's exactly how we feel. We don't mind sharing with those little feather dusters you think are so darned cute, but they need an attitude adjustment. They think they deserve equal time at the trough.

It is not a squirrel's goal in life to stress out people who feed birds. Our lives are on cruise control. We seldom think more than ten minutes ahead of time. We used to be able to find all the natural food we needed before the suburbs moved to the country to live with us. You can take a squirrel out of the country, but you can't take the country out of the squirrel. We realize our presence does not make some people happy. They see us at the feeder and get bound up tighter than a wax doll's eardrum.

At first we thought all this seed offering was an apology for cutting down all our trees. Now, it has been made very clear the seed is not meant for us at all and going to the feeder makes us nervous as a sparrow at a hawk convention. Things get so bad that occasionally we sometimes think about going back to a natural food diet. Feeders are becoming so sophisticated that it takes us half a day just to case the joint. Some Ph.D. in rodent architectural design thinks he can short-circuit millions of years of squirrel genetic engineering. That's corn syrup. It will never happen. We have never tried to force our intentions on anyone. Even though we have become very fond of birdfeed, we follow the rules of engagement in our continued battle to occupy the territory that is rightfully ours. We were here long before these suburbanites arrived with their pink flamingos. We have never resorted to physical attacks. Our efforts have always been solely psychological.

Rehabilitation is no longer an option. Every reformed seed addict I can think of has fallen hopelessly back into the black hole of black oil sunflower seed. We have tried to convince young squirrels not to experiment with birdseed, but the stuff is so available it is a constant temptation. A lot of young squirrels get hooked on cracked corn. Once they do crack there is nothing stopping them from becoming unproductive, wasted individuals.

The new wave of a squirrel-equipment-buying public and the products they bring home is very confusing. Squirrel bashing still seems to be in fashion when people gather to talk birdfeeding, yet many people are finding they can't live without us. When we accept birdseed, we have no intention of being domesticated. Even in those rare times when no one chases us, we feel it is important to stay in shape and preserve our wild animal heritage. That's why we're slippin', slidin', peepin' and hidin' when we leave a birdfeeder. This sends a mixed message to those who have always been understanding and willing to share their birdseed with us. But we are not about to be turned into docile, hand-fed, furry-faced, pudgy pacifists. We are radical rodents ready to reap whatever is sown. We ask no permission, take none for granted.

We taught Euell Gibbons everything he knew. If push comes to shove and we are ever baffled by bourgeois bird feeders, we can still survive because we have not lost our guerilla warfare tactical training. We can still forage in the foliage. But don't get me wrong. We are going to ride this new wave of squirrel popularity as long as we can. Some of the new contraptions, like those cute little chairs with the spiked corn tables, have improperly sized seating for full-figured squirrels, but we will cope.

We consider ourselves equal opportunity annoyers. As nice as some folks can be to us, we are still happier than a gopher in soft dirt when we can destroy a new birdfeeder. Looking in a kitchen window and watching people go berserk because I am having a bite to eat — now that's entertainment!

I have had a lot of hurdles to get over in my life, emotional ups and downs, and obstacles in my path to success. But I have always found an inner drive (and sometimes overdrive) to keep me motivated and upbeat. It would have been easy to throw my paws up in the air and quit when so many people wanted to see me fail, but that is just not my style.

Hairy Houdini

Let Nature scold the hawk that kills the jay,
The jay that destroys the wren's nest,
The wren that pierces the robin's egg,
The robin that eats the worm,
It is her way!   —Dick E. Bird

1•

The Basics

Think of Your Birdfeeder as a Fine Restaurant

You want to run your birdfeeding program just like you would a
fine restaurant. Your birds are looking for the same things you are
when you go out to eat: good fresh food, friendly service, a clean
environment, a menu choice with a little variety, a nice view, comfortable seating—and make sure there's enough water. Don't forget
that you have to advertise until you have a steady clientele. After
that others will hear by word of beak. To begin, put out feeders
with lots of seed visibility. Remember, birds can't smell the stuff.
Like any good restaurant, you have to lure them in with delectable
appetizers like suet, fruit, nuts, nectar, and even a few crushed
egg shells to give your birds some true grit. They need grit to
digest all the other goodies you give them. The responsibility to
keep those birds coming back for more is entirely on your shoul-

1

ders, and the way to do that is to make sure your birdfeeders are full and clean. This is one of the most important things that you must remember when opening a birdfeeder. The returns your birds will give you are immeasurable.

You Are What You Eat

If this were true most birders would look like chocolate-covered donuts, and I know my birds would look like sunflower seeds. There are all kinds of foods out there for birds, from bugs to birdseed. Whoever said, "There is no such thing as a free lunch," never met my birds or my resident squirrel, Hairy Houdini. Birds can process a huge amount of food because of their high rate of metabolism. Have you ever seen a fat bird? Squirrels are a different story. Squirrels gain weight very fast. The first place it begins to show is in the face. This is also true with humans. The reason is that both species can fill their cheeks full of food without swallowing. With man and squirrels, food seldom spends much time in the stomach. It often just goes from cheek to cheek.

Many people would be surprised to find that the seed they put out is only a small portion of their birds' total diet. Even if you spent 100 percent of your income on birdseed, birds would only rely on you for about 20 percent of their diet. Songbirds live basically on a natural food diet of vegetation, insects and smaller neighbors. Your feeders are an incentive for birds to visit you. Those of you who think they stop by because they're sincerely interested in a relationship should reevaluate the seed bill. You are being used. Your birds are gold diggers. If you didn't have seed, they wouldn't give you a second look. If you can't take care of them in the style they are accustomed to, they will find someone who will! But, if you're like me, it's all worth the abuse you have to endure, because birds are the most intriguing piece in nature's puzzle.

There is no reason to bore your birds with a limited menu. Most feed stores, garden centers, and wild bird-related outlets carry a huge assortment of feeding choices. If you still aren't satisfied, or your birds are finicky, you can try some homemade recipes: nectar, suet, peanut mixes, fruit, bread, crushed dog food, dried melon seeds, homegrown berries, and my favorite—weeds. I have found that letting the yard go to weeds makes the birds very happy and saves me hours and hours of chasing a lawn mower.

Let your birds worry about the balance of their diet. You just keep supplying them with everything you can afford, deliver promptly, and make sure you only supply quality product. Then you will have a clientele of birds that will entertain you from sunup to sundown.

Use Your Bird Sense

Backyard birdfeeding can be very enjoyable, and you don't have to work real hard at it. By following a few common-sense methods, you can actually invite the types of birds you enjoy most. The best way is to experiment with varied heights and locations for your feeding stations. Use hanging and post-mounted feeders. Try thinking like a bird. Visibility is very important because birds find seed through sight. The eyeball tells the brain, and the brain tells the wing. Before you know it, they are perched right there on the birdfeeder filling their faces.

Provide your birds with some quick cover. They want to come for dinner, not *be* dinner. Nature is a rough neighborhood, so be careful where you place your feeder stations. The best locations are within darting distance to natural cover.

Consider the convenience of filling your feeders. If you have an active backyard of birds, you may have to fill feeders quite often. If you are five-foot-two, don't mount your feeder seven and a half feet high unless you have a very tall spouse.

Backyard Fling

I am often asked why so many people find it important to feed wild birds. Is there not enough natural food to go around? The answer to the natural food question is usually yes. In most areas wild birds can eke out an existence on what Mother Nature provides. (So could you for that matter, but I usually see most of you in the cookie aisle at the grocery store.) The food we provide is often a welcome energy source for our backyard buddies who are often already stressed in many ways by loss of habitat and continual change to their environment, over which they have no control.

"No, thanks. I packed a lunch!"

The majority of us feed our wild birds because we want them close. They are a source of enjoyment that continually entertains and amazes us. Those who contend that birds can find all they need in the wild, fail to mention that it might be a little hard to find *the wild* anymore. What happens if you're a bird and your wild turns into a planned-unit development? The first thing I'd do is head straight for a yard full of birdfeeders and settle down.

We feed birds for many reasons, but one has to be an inner need to come close to nature, to experience its complex simplicity, and to take an appreciation from it. What we put out for them not only fills out their diet but also feeds our soul with a much-needed reminder that we, too, are a part of this circle called life.

It is estimated that 100 million people are feeding wild birds in North America. It is the fastest growing pastime of the last two decades. If you are not one of these people, you might want to see a psychiatrist because you are surely not normal. If you are one of those hard-nosed holdouts who says birds should only eat natural food, then get out there and plant them some!

Just Meat and Potatoes

It's really nice to have a lot of neat gadgets to feed your birds with and keep your squirrels entertained, but nothing is actually a necessity when it comes to birdfeeding. To bring the birds in, all you have to do is offer them something they enjoy eating. It's fun to have all the fancy dispensers, but I know a lot of fishermen with boxes full of lures and bait and no fish. The same can be said about backyard birdfeeders. You can have all the gear, but no birds. Actually, feeders are like fishing lures. You use them to bring in the birds. But the only way to get them to bite is with lots of good food. There are many different lures for many different birds, but like fish, some will bite on anything.

A cup of seed on a wide kitchen window ledge will bring in a variety of birds, but that is not always practical. The many different

"Would you like to leave your name? There is about a three-hour wait."

5

feeders on the market today help fine-tune feeding practices. Many are designed to make it more convenient to fill and maintain. Some have been developed to make it easier to observe and feed.

All your birds ask for is a little effort on your part. If your feeding establishment is held up often by a bandit with a bushy tail and a face full of fur, your birds will understand. If they find out you are just unreliable, irresponsible, and inconsistent, it won't matter how fancy your feeders are. It will be—bye, bye, birdies.

Multiplication Tables

If you want tons of birds in your yard, you just need to use some simple arithmetic. The most agreed-upon equation is: double your feeders in order to triple your birds. You may not buy this theory, but it works. Put a single tray on a pole and heap it with food for a couple days. Notice the activity and then put out a second feed station offering a different seed choice or more choices of suet and fruit. Don't get carried away; this equation is not like the national debt—it has a ceiling. Variety and location are important, as they will not only increase overall numbers but also species. This method also cuts down on traffic jams around your feeders and helps reduce friction.

To make your feeding program work the way you want it to, decide what birds you would like to attract and try to duplicate their natural food needs as much as possible. If you feed birds regularly, your feeder will quickly become very grungy. *Obligation No. 1*, clean your feeder well and clean it often. You do the dishes after every meal don't you? Birds like to eat off clean dishes as well. How about a drink? Ever take a bath? *Obligation No. 2*, give them lots of good, clean water. Where do you put your feeders? *Obligation No. 3*, give them shelter. Put your feeders close to some bushes or tree cover where the birds can make a quick getaway.

When you are sure all of these duties are completed, feel free to go to work, or whatever else you enjoy doing. Remember, only you can prevent empty birdfeeders.

If you are just beginning and not sure which seeds your birds will like, just remember: beggars can't be choosers. I suggest you start out with striped and black-oil sunflower seeds, white millet, cracked corn, and niger thistle. It will not take long to see who goes for what and what goes the quickest. Black-oil seed usually gets eaten first since most birds prefer it. Whatever you do, don't get caught with your seed down. Birds are not the most loyal friends you will ever have. If your neighbor is feeding better quality stuff than you are, you can just kiss your birds good-bye. The way to a bird's heart is through his stomach. If you are trying to pass some cheap, inferior seed off on your birds, they will get wise to you very quickly. Word travels fast in the treetops, and it doesn't take long for you to get on the used-birdseed list if you're not careful.

Wet Those Whistles

One of the greatest things about birdfeeding is that it takes little skill and hardly any equipment. Just by offering food, shelter, and water to your birds, you can begin a relationship that is rewarding to you and to them. As you begin to gain knowledge of your birds' needs, you can begin to adjust your feeding techniques. You will then start to realize that different birds have different needs.

> *A seed saved is a bird lost.*

Water is often the most neglected part of attracting birds to your yard, especially in the winter. Many people clean out their birdbaths in the fall and store them away, but winter is actually the most important time of the year to supply your birds with H_2O because it is much harder to come by. Besides drinking the stuff, birds need a water supply for bathing purposes. Believe it or not, birds bathe to keep warm. All birds need to keep their feathers clean or they will not provide the insulation and warmth they are designed so well for. Never put an additive in your birdbath to keep it from freezing. Any additive you use will restrict flight and mat feathers, causing hypothermia.

Several years ago, a major magazine suggested to its millions of readers that they put glycerine in their birdbaths to keep them from freezing during the winter months. It was an honest mistake. The writer had visited her feed dealer just before finalizing the story and the feed dealer suggested she put glycerine in her birdbath to keep it from freezing. He told her this is what farmers do to keep water troughs from freezing over. I called the magazine and explained that ingesting glycerine would not harm birds but it would create mini oil-spills in birdbaths, matting feathers, restricting flight and in severe cases cause hypothermia. The magazine couldn't retract the article for several months, so I called Paul Harvey and he told the whole world not to do it. But every year, just as winter begins in the northern tier states and people are considering their birdbath options, the idea raises its ugly head again. Outdoor writers looking for subject matter seem to retrieve that piece of misinformation regularly. *The only additive you want in your birdbath is water—two parts H, one part O!*

"I would like the special. Just put it on my bill."

Letting your sprinkler run during dry weather will attract many sunbird bathers. Birds love water sprinklers. It is the main reason so many of them have moved to the suburbs.

To Feed or Not to Feed? That is the Question

There are two types of people in this world: those who feed their birds and those who do not. You, believe it or not, are one of these people. Now, if you are Type A, you already know that it doesn't cost that much money to share a little cracked corn cuisine with your wild birds. If you're Type B, my guess is you're so tight that when you wink your kneecaps wiggle.

I'm here to tell you that buying birdseed will not break you. When you get to the cash register, have the cashier go through your stash very slowly and keep your eyes glued to the subtotal. If you begin to go over-budget, start slashing nonessentials—like toilet paper or cat food. While we're on the subject, get rid of the cat; he's just using you. If you're at the garden center, there are any number of things you can do without. Scratch the flower bulbs; you'll get your knees dirty burying them, and they don't come up half the time anyway.

"Have you seen the rake, Bea?"

I think I have heard all the arguments against feeding birds. Feeding extends their range, it creates an

9

unnatural dependency, the agricultural process of growing bird-seed displaces natural habitat, and it entices birds to congregate in large numbers creating possible health-related problems. There is some truth to all these arguments but they are of little importance when compared to all the other harvesting and management practices we levy on the environment that directly impact our wild birds.

> *May your birds never know want until the seed is at hand!*

So if you're still on the fence over this issue, remember: a farmer never plowed a field by turning it over in his mind. Abraham Lincoln did not become president because he was born in a log cabin, but because he got out of it and filled his feeders. Benjamin Franklin hung his birdfeeder out right after signing the Declaration of Independence and said to the other founding fathers, "We must all hang together, else we shall all hang separately."

Your birds can be very agreeable friends; they ask no questions and make no criticism.

The Three Very Important Poles

There are three very important poles on this good Earth: the North Pole, the South Pole, and the Birdfeeder Pole. These three poles help in stabilizing the world because birds range from the North Pole to the South Pole and to all the birdfeeder poles inbetween. Most birds would not turn down a good meal offered from a hanging feeder, but 90 percent of those we surveyed claimed they would choose a pole-mounted feeder over a hanging feeder any day. A better way to understand how birds feel about hanging feeders is to eat dinner in a rocking chair. To get the full effect, hold the tray with one hand and eat with your other while you rock back and forth — at least two round trips every five seconds.

Most birds prefer a pole equipped with a squirrel baffle. We found that the majority of birds hate waiting in line behind a fat squirrel. You may want to consider a swinging baffle for your feeder pole, depending on the skill level of your squirrels.

The Need to Feed

Many people question whether feeding year-round is necessary or not. Some would argue that there is enough natural food in the summer so feeder visitations will be reduced during that season. On the other hand, you can expect the largest variety of birds in the summer months.

As much as I put out, they should be hooked on the stuff by now. I even think my squirrel has a two-pound-a-day habit.

If you think adding a few scoops of seed to your feeder is too strenuous an activity for you, perhaps you should consider another less active hobby, like sleeping. But if you're just lazy you might want to put out larger quantities of feed to cut down on the number of trips you take to the backyard. There are some feeders on the market that will hold thirty to fifty pounds. That amount will easily last an hour or so.

Just the Necessities

How many times have you heard that line? Are you afraid to send your bird crazy spouse to the feed store alone? Do you cringe when the garden center owner comes out smiling, and says, "Don't you worry. We deliver big orders free." In many cases this can be a nerve-racking experience, but birdfeeding is completely different. I cannot think of a nicer way to go broke. Some people gamble their money away while others spend it on frivolous material things like clothes, a car to drive back and forth to work, or tuition for their children's education.

11

Buffer Zone

I heard it in the hedgerow, in the neighbor's yard;
A bird I'd never heard before, I listened very hard.
I crouched so low and crept so soft, I traumatized the cat;
He, too, had heard this lovely bird, and knew where it was at.
I used the cat and all his skill to point me on my way;
Then with assumed seniority, convinced him not to stay.
Again, I moved toward the sound, whittling the gap;
Peering through the hedgerow, the sound my only map.
But then a silence filtered in, no longer any sound;
A stillness overtook me, as I sat and glanced around.
Then movement through the tangled leaves, slight but just enough;
And eye contact in shocked surprise, with my neighbor in the buff.
I can't explain, the bird had flown, the cat only assisted;
And now I can't enjoy my birds, my neighbors think I'm twisted.
— *Dick E. Bird*

If you have funneled a good share of your hard-earned money into feeding the birds in your backyard, you already know the many benefits those dollars pay back to you. If you are just getting started in backyard birdfeeding, the first thing to remember is: Always go shopping for birdfeed on an empty stomach. It has been proven in test after test that people who buy on an empty stomach always load up on goodies twice as much as those who have just eaten. If you were to go to the feed supplier after a big meal, you would most likely not buy enough birdfeed. The rule of thumb for buying birdfeed is fifty pounds of seed, suet, and nectar per year for each bird you count within two miles of your house. When it comes to equipment, you never know what your birds might prefer, so buy one of each item you think might tickle their fancy.

Actually, buying birdseed in fifty-pound bags is your best economy, because you pay a premium for smaller amounts. There are a zillion birdfeeders on the market and chances are your birds have seen them all. The feeders you choose will certainly cause your birds to form an opinion of you, and first impressions are very important. So I cannot stress enough the point about choosing a feeder carefully. Visibility, capacity, and accessibility are all very important factors to consider. Advertising can be misleading, so it's important to make your own decisions. Consider the fact that there are over two dozen mountains in Colorado taller than Pikes Peak, yet you don't know the names of any of them. When you make a purchase, you must think like the bird you want to attract. This does not mean flitting around the store in an indecisive manner; you will only upset the manager.

> *Filling the birdfeeder is its own reward.*

What Goes Up Must Fall Down— Preventative Feeder Maintenance.

When your birdfeeder is in need of repair or maintenance, the first thing you should do is bring it inside and clean it. After it has thoroughly dried, get your tools. They're in the kitchen drawer with the mismatched nails, jar lids, sardine keys, tongue depressors, used birthday candles, and snarled string. If the drawer will not open, it is because you jammed it shut the last time you were in there and this junk tends to rise like bread once the drawer is closed.

If you use an adhesive to repair your feeder, remember that different adhesives are used for different materials (except fingers—all glue sticks to fingers). Make sure you use a good moisture-resistant adhesive. Many late-model birdfeeders are constructed of plastic and can be repaired with epoxy. Many manufacturers offer repair kits that include those feeder parts most often digested by squirrels.

Don't wait until your birdfeeder falls apart before you work on it. If you keep the feeder full, you'll need a squirrel patch soon enough.

Repairing the birdfeeder can be a pleasant change from the usually boring jobs around the house. Keeping the feeder clean will ensure that your spouse doesn't throw it out. Serious bird feeders spend hours repairing their feeders because they're not that bright and they're too cheap to buy another one.

It is much better to start out with a birdfeeder made from material you are familiar working with. Many of the plastic feeders are difficult to repair without a plastic extrusion machine to replace the parts the squirrels chewed to pieces.

When you finally get around to cleaning and repairing your feeders, don't take a week to do it. You have a lot of customers who are not used to waiting for their food. Before taking the feeder down, look it over, decide what must be done, what materials you will need, cost estimates, time studies, environmental-impact report, a quick check of the safety rules, and then see if you can get that darned kitchen drawer open.

Punctuality

Some say the problem with being punctual is that no one is there to appreciate it. This is not the case with your birds. They develop a rhythm if they are regular visitors to your birdfeeders. If you're there on time, they will always be waiting in the wings. If you are inconsistent in your feeding habits, they will be inconsistent in their visiting habits. Like all wild things, birds follow the laws of nature. It is a survival creed that is heeded by all wild things. It is as structured as ours but much more swift in consequence.

Take a Gander

Scrambling for the binoculars is not the norm when yet another chicka-dee flies in, but perhaps there is rea-

Feed now or forever hold your seed.

son to put the scope on your repeat customers. You can learn a lot more about what your investment in seed, suet, feeders, and time is doing by watching the birds that are enjoying them. Recognizing the wild birds in your backyard is a good first step. That way you do not have to call them "little brown, yellow, or

"Who are those guys?"

red birds," and you get to know their personalities. Your birds might even start to question their own self-worth if you do not call them by their given names.

An excellent way of getting to know your birds is to use the binoculars more often. Study their feeding habits, preening methods, how they cock their heads and twitch their tails. There is a purpose for everything these creatures do. To survive, birds must be organized in their every movement. In the nest, if you're slow, you don't grow. Many birds eat their weight in food each day while trying not to be eaten. If you put the binoculars on them more often, you will notice the intense look on their faces. It is the same look you see in the face of a floor trader on the commodity exchange. A bird is wondering about its next meal while it is swallowing the one it has. Grab the binocs. See for yourself.

Who Are Those Guys?

Often, when a bird you have never seen before shows up at your feeder, you become very excited and run all over the house looking for the binoculars—which are always in the last place you look. When you finally get to the window, six blue jays will most

15

likely be there, smiling back at you. Identifying birds can sometimes be very difficult. If you cannot get them to produce some ID, it is wise to look quickly for prominent field marks, color variations, beak size, shape and length, flight pattern, and, most importantly, song or call. Many birds that show up at your feeder are very common, but they will only be common to you if you pay attention to them. Listening to your birds is a lot like learning a second language. If you can add a birdsong to your hearing vocabulary every once in a while, it won't be long before you are fluent in the language of birds. Remember, you never learn anything by talking. Sit and listen to what your birds have to say. If your memory is as strong as your credit at the feed store, you should be able to identify your birds before you ever see them. They all have calling cards, and once you get plugged into the backyard airwaves people are going to start thinking you are a natural genius.

If you have gone through six field guides, two sets of bird-sound tapes, your collection of U.S. postage stamps commemorating birds, and you still cannot identify what the heck you are feeding every day, don't be upset. There are actually several species of whatchamacallits in North America that never have been properly recorded in the currently available field guides. They are often nondescript birds that make very little sound and have few bad habits. It is believed that Eastern and Western whatchamacallits interbreed, which complicates things even further. Their sporadic range is not well defined and food preferences seem to be nonexistent. Most likely, the bird or birds that you are unable to identify are one or more of these whatchamacallits.

Winging It
Given the time of year, there are four basic groups of birds that will visit you. Depending on your location, these groups are per-

manent residents, summer residents, winter residents, or visitors. You can categorize the different groups by taking notice of their stay with you. Some you will see the whole year-round, while others only take up residence during the nesting season and then head for the sunny South. Many might be winter residents only, since they spend their summers in the far North. Last but not least, my favorites, the transients. I always give these nomads special treatment. It doesn't matter who your nomads are; when you see them migrating through, put out a little extra for them, since they are traveling and need the energy.

Some of your birds will leave and not even say good-bye. So subtle is their movement that they are gone before you realize it. A few will be replaced by those who choose to spend the winter with you and share your offerings with those permanent standby customers you see every day, come rain or shine.

You can use your imagination to think of all the interesting places your summer visitors fly to when it turns to winter. Many of the hummingbirds you have cared for all summer will wing their way over the Panama Canal; your orioles might go to the Andes; your barn swallows to Argentina. We begin to understand how small the world we live in really is.

The dangers our migrating birds face worsen every year. Stop-over areas they have used for millions of years become developed, poisoned by agricultural runoff, dried up, or flooded. Before we ever figure out what causes migration, how the birds are guided, and how they actually disperse themselves, we risk losing them completely.

What Good Are Songbirds?

If you need reasons for their existence, other than their melodious song and beautiful plumage, there are many. Even the non-appreciator of wild birds should be thankful for the roles they play in the renewal of life. Through the variety of their intriguing habits, songsters replenish fields and forests by distributing seed, pollinating plants, controlling insect populations and pushing the economy to new highs by eating millions of tons of wildbird seed annually.

We can thank these creatures for eating the mosquitoes and grasshoppers before mosquitoes and grasshoppers eat us. Birds are incredible creatures that spread joy wherever they roam. Many a bird dropping has turned into a berry bush seedling. Since most weed seed eaters fully digest all seeds they consume, dispersal of weed seeds by birds is not widespread.

The Big Three

Whether you are a city dweller or a country bumpkin, you must consider the same things when planning landscaping for your birds. Your birds need three basic elements to survive and be content in your backyard: cover for protection from natural and unnatural enemies and elements, safe areas that enable them to reproduce and bear their young; and reliable food and water sources. You can plant vegetation that is ideal for nesting sites as well as natural food sources such as serviceberry and juniper. If you plan carefully, with the help of your local nursery, you can actually select your plants to provide the maximum overlap of flowering and fruiting times. It is not necessary to plant a jungle in your backyard to attract birds to your window. Birdfeeders alone will bring you some results, but birds will always require natural food sources no matter how much seed you supply. By providing these natural food sources and protective cover, your yard will attract a wider variety of birds and make them much closer friends.

Developing a bird-friendly habitat in your yard will increase your property value. I'm not making this stuff up. Studies have shown that property values rise 4 to 11 percent with the addition of vegetation and tree cover. The habitat that you create will be pleasing to you and your wildlife. Whether you believe it or not, you are interconnected with everything else in nature, and with a little sweat equity you can maintain contact with some of the friendliest creatures ever to fly the friendly skies.

Are Dummies Stupid?

People spend a lot of time and money perching fake owls on their property and placing fake snakes in their gardens to scare off unwanted birds. Some experts feel that birds are very slow-witted and cannot even tell if another bird is alive or dead, and can only distinguish sex through behavior.

Will an owl with a mute hoot scare anything away? Not often. I have seen sparrows nested on the head of an owlequin. I have seen people, who forgot they placed fake snakes in their gardens, jump and jump many more times just ahead of their brooms because they forgot to tell their spouses they were there. If "intelligence" is defined strictly by actions, we are all suspiciously lacking. Perhaps "intelligence" is better defined by experimentation. Birds, like man, are very inquisitive.

I have watched crows mob a plastic roosting owl in the middle of the day. I assume they thought it was the real McCoy but perhaps they were only practicing.

As for the difference between a mute owl and a hoot owl, how many times have you bought clothing that looked good on a store dummy? I'm not talking about the one inside trying to sell you the stuff—I mean the one in the window. If you watch people, they will stand at the window and imagine themselves wearing these fancy duds. If they look good on one dummy, why not another? This is no different from a crow mob-

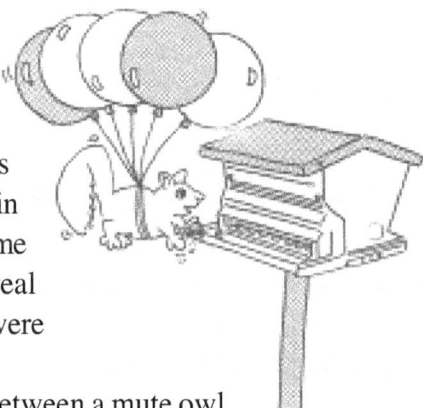

19

bing an owl with rigormortis. The bird is simply imagining himself as a fearless defender of his tribe.

I Can't Believe They Ate the Whole Thing!
Half of feeding birds is dealing with squirrels. This book will not only teach you how to manage your birdseed, but it will also show you how your squirrels will manage you.

After years of research, it is a well-documented fact that squirrels' eyes are much bigger than their stomachs. The nerve endings between the stomach and the brain are poorly developed. This causes the squirrel to eat far beyond his capacity before the brain actually receives the message to shut down the jaw muscles. There are good points to having mobs of hoarding rodents visit your bird-feeder on a regular basis. The main advantage is that you never have to clean the feeder. Any squirrel worth his seed will usually destroy a birdfeeder long before it ever has a chance to become dirty. Sharks feed in a frenzy, but squirrels feed in a frantic.

The one thing most squirrels have going for them is the fact that they get plenty of exercise. They lead very busy lives and can actually burn off calories while they are eating. If you study your squirrels, you will notice their jaws seem to move faster than the wings of a hummingbird. This constant rapid motion takes an enormous amount of energy. It takes one sunflower seed out of every two just to fuel the jaw muscles that process the tons of intake a squirrel annually digests. Most squirrels can hold twice their own weight in each cheek, which distorts the face considerably, causing them to look congested. A munching squirrel is unable to close his eyelids because the facial tissue is stretched too far, restricting lid actuation, and causing the eyes to look bigger than the stomach.

You Must Deal with the Doo!

I often hear the same handful of negative gripes about feeding birds that quite honestly do not have easy solutions.

Some people will tell you that there is an easy solution for everything that ails you. At one time these people were called "Snake Oil" salesmen. Today, we call them experts.

The fact is, many birdfeeding gripes can't be fixed with just the snap of a finger. If you feed birds seed wrapped in hulls, the hulls are yours. The birds, in most cases, will leave them for you to clean up.

Where birds congregate, you will find droppings. They also leave that for you to clean up. Please do.

Predators will always be attracted to areas where birds congregate, and the birdbath will have ring around the collar. Only you can do something about these things—deal with it.

Do you get the picture? It's just a little bit of responsibility you trade for a whole lot of enjoyment.

Birdfeeding Etiquette:

Q: *How long does a hostess have to wait for tardy birds to find the feeder?*
A: Formal rules of feeder etiquette state that the host or hostess must wait as long as it takes for guests to arrive. It is very important to make sure the invitation is clear.

Q: *Should the suet be placed on the right or left side of the seed at an informal feeding station?*
A: At an informal feeding station it makes no difference on which side the suet is placed. However, the water must always be within easy reach of each guest.

Q: *Should one knock before politely asking a squirrel to leave the feeder or simply and quietly chase after it?*
A: It is not appropriate to chase after any rodent which has crashed a dinner party. A rapid, forceful window knock is the correct action to take. If this does not stimulate the correct response, then — and only then — is a chase in order.

Q: *What is the correct way to fill a birdfeeder? Must one use a scoop or is it appropriate to use one's fingers?*
A: It really depends upon the time, place and company. The general rule for filling the birdfeeder is to use a scoop whenever possible. If no one is looking, you can just grab the seed with your hands and shove it in.

Q: *What is the proper attire to be worn to the birdfeeder?*
A: The only fashion concern here is to be overdressed in the summer, or under-dressed in the winter. The rules of etiquette do not call for elaborate and ornate outerwear, but comfortable underwear is advised.

Recap and Reinforce:

• Every minute you put off filling the feeder your birds lose 60 seconds of happiness.

• For more than seventy years researchers have been banding birds. Over 50 million bands have been attached to birds of all kinds. Only about 3 million have been returned. Those of you holding the remaining 47 million had better start turning them in. This isn't funny anymore.

• The more expensive the birdfeeder, the less often you will be able to afford to fill it.

• Birdbath heaters only break down in cold weather.

• A bird that sings nonstop all morning will not make a peep when you go to look for it.

• Birds spend a great amount of time on feather care because it is their primary source of protection from the elements and their key to flight.

• Approximately 650 species of birds breed in North America.

• Often birds will sleep standing on one of their legs. This does not mean one leg is asleep. They crank up half their landing gear to conserve energy in cold weather. Their featherless feet and legs can lose a lot of heat just standing there acting like a kick-stand, so they get a leg up on the situation and try to show as little leg as possible.

• Place fruit offerings away from seed offerings. Many birds that will be attracted to fruit will tend to shy away from all the activity at the seeder feeder.

Dear Dick E. Bird

Dear Dick E. Bird:

Since retiring, my husband now gets up at 5 o'clock every morning to fill his many birdfeeders around the yard. Before he goes out he makes toast and coffee (which happens to be located directly under the smoke detector). He slams the door on the way out and leaves the TV blasting the early-morning Farm Report. He spends a large chunk of our retirement nest-egg on multiple varieties of wild birdseed and feeding stations. None of this bothers me too much except when he goes out in the morning he's naked as a jaybird except for his boots. Please tell me what I should do as the neighbors are beginning to talk.

—Early Bird in Baltimore

Dear Early Bird:

These are all symptoms of retirement readjustment. My suggestion is to be patient and perhaps invest in an expensive pair of earplugs. You may want to sew his pantlegs to his boots until his routine includes putting on his pants automatically. I have heard similar accounts and, I assure you, it gets worse before it gets better. He will soon start telling you how to do your grocery shopping. Just send him off to the feed store.

—Keep Smilin', Dick E. Bird

Dear Dick E. Bird:

I have always heard birds are very light eaters. Is this true?

— Tweeter Feeder in Toronto

Dear Tweeter:

Yes, this is very true. In fact, most birds start eating at first light and don't stop until moonlight. Birds eat enormous amounts of food compared to their total body weight. Roosting birds, it has been discovered, actually dream about eating. You don't have to worry about how much to feed your birds, just pile it on and they will never say "when."

— Keep Smilin', Dick E. Bird

Tongue-in-Beak Tidbits

If you want to graduate in the top 10 percent of your class, do not go on to the next chapter until you have mastered this one.

APPLY FEATHERED FACTS:
1. When a squirrel gains weight, where is the first place it begins to show?
2. Can your birds smell your seed offerings?
3. How much of a bird's diet does your seed actually account for?

DISCUSSION TOPICS:
1. Should you use additives to keep the water in your birdbath from freezing?
2. Are you saving birds by feeding them?
3. What is the best way to increase your property value?

4. What is the most important food source for birds?

5. What do we find woven into our lives through religion, philosophy, song, poetry, science, folklore, myth, superstition, art and weather forecasting?

BIRD-BRAINED TRIVIA STUDY:

1. Where do birds come from?

2. On which side does a bird have the most feathers?

3. What do scientists feel is the greatest threat to birds and wildlife today?

4. What is considered the best brain food for birds?

5. Why do birds fly south in the winter?

AND THE ANSWER IS—

Apply Feathered Facts: 1. In his face. 2. No, birds do not smell very good. 3. About 20 percent. **Discussion Topics:** 1. Absolutely not. 2. No, your return on investment is enjoying them up close and personal. 3. Planting wildlife habitat. 4. Insects. 5. Birds. **Bird-Brained Trivia:** 1. Birdseed. 2. Outside. 3. Loss of habitat. 4. Bookworms. 5. It's too far to walk!

*Nature is so gentle she can hold a humming-
bird to the nectar without disturbing the
loose petal of a flower and wear down a
mountain in the silence of time.*

—Dick E. Bird

2•

Fine—Tuning

Birdfeeding Helps Lift the Human Spirit

Birdfeeding is a pastime that is continually attracting new fans. It is
probably more common in rural and suburban areas than in large
cities, but even the metropolitan areas with their many high-rise
apartments offer the opportunity to feed wild birds. Next time
you're in the car, take notice of the number of yards with
birdfeeders. You will be amazed by the many houses that have
some type of seed dispenser on the property.

Traditionally, most folks would feed during the winter months,
but now the trend is to feed year-round. Many people spend
$200 or more a year on seed for their backyard birds. In many
cases, feeding wild birds is the only day-to-day contact people
have with their surrounding natural world. It enables them to enjoy nature at its finest, right from their kitchen windows.

When You Buy a Birdfeeder, Think Like a Bird!

Does it keep the seed dry? Is the seed easily accessed? Does the hopper hold five hundred pounds of seed? It is surprising how many people buy feeders because they look fancy. There are a lot of good birdfeeders on the market today, so deciding which ones are right for you depends on what you already have, how much you want to spend, and how many birds you want to attract. The most important consideration is whether or not birds can see the food that is in the bird-feeder. If birds can't actually see the seed you're offering, the only animal that will know it's there is Hairy Houdini. Other factors to consider are: capacity, easy-fill openings, secure assembly, easy-cleaning design, weather protection, proper perching areas, price, mounting method, and, most importantly, does it make you tingle inside when you think of owning it? The unit can have all the gadgets in the world, but if it doesn't make you tingle, you should hang on to your jingle.

There are simple methods you can apply when trying to keep larger birds off your feeders and allow only small songbirds. You can modify the tube feeders you have by shortening the perches or taking them off completely. The small songbirds will still cling to the openings and feed. You can also screen your feeder's visitors with small wire openings that allow only certain sized birds in, and there are adjust-

"Hold still, Bea.
I'm spilling the seed."

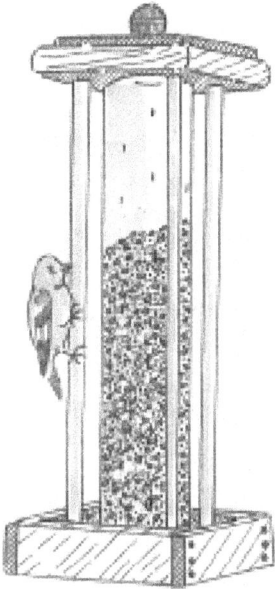

Vertical perch
thistle seed feeder

able dome feeders that permit only smaller birds to flutter up into them. You determine the opening size.

You can control the lunch crowd by controlling the competition.

As seed volume drops in a tube feeder, the higher perched openings go out of business. Look for a feeder with the openings close to the bottom, so your seating capacity does not dwindle as the seed is consumed.

Many feeders have metal feeding ports that will help slow down squirrel damage, but you will find you can never underestimate a furball. Eventually, you will notice gnaw marks growing, like a fungus around the metal feeder ports, until one morning you'll find a gaping hole and no seed.

Feeders that dispense thistle seed have dozens of small openings that allow small finches to access the seed, while at the same time discouraging the larger birds. One unique design is the vertical perched thistle feeder.

Man is never so tall as when he is out filling his birdfeeder.

Goldfinches feed naturally on weed seeds. Since weeds do not have perches, the birds must eat while clinging to the weed stalk. The four vertical perches on verticle thistle feeders allow them to perch naturally. I have seen as many as thirty-five finches stacked up at a time, filling their faces.

Is there truly a squirrel-proof birdfeeder? I wouldn't bet any money on it. Some designs might slow squirrels down, but they will come in on stilts or hang gliders if they have to—and eventually they will eat your seed!

Feeder Installation

You can use a threaded pipe and pipe flange to mount your birdfeeder or birdhouse. But unless you have some plumbing material around the house, you will find the cost of buying these items as expensive as purchasing a commercially packaged pole designed specifically for feeder/house mounting. (This could be a profitable sideline for plumbers.) A pipe flange screws onto the bottom of the feeder/house and has inside threads so that it then can be attached to a length of threaded pipe. A good rule of thumb is to buy the smallest-diameter pipe that will still be rigid enough to handle the load you intend to place on it, plus 127 pounds of squirrels. You will find poles much more durable and easier to baffle than posts. Poles will thwart squirrels with no athletic ability. When you buy a length of pipe, don't forget that some of it has to go into the ground.

Pipe flange

There are hundreds of squirrel-baffling devices on the market, but none of them will work any better than a thirty-pound fruit tin turned upside down on your feeder pole just under the birdfeeder.

30

Love Thy Squirrelly Neighbor

I looked out through the blinding snow,
To see what I could see.
And bulgy cheeks and beady eyes,
Were looking back at me.
I didn't yell and rant and rave,
Or try to make it flee.
That face in all its innocence said,
"I thought this stuff was free."
— *Dick E. Bird*

If you want to discourage squirrels by hanging your birdfeeder from a solid object, do not use nylon fishing line. Rubber-coated cord material will work almost as well and will be more visible to birds. Many injuries are caused from birds flying into wires, and using a visible line is the only way to prevent this. You have to go out on a limb for most hanging feeders to work. Go out far enough so that your squirrel cannot jump to the feeder. Let the feeder hang down to just where you can reach it to fill it comfortably. Most squirrels will accept the challenge, but by the time they hit the

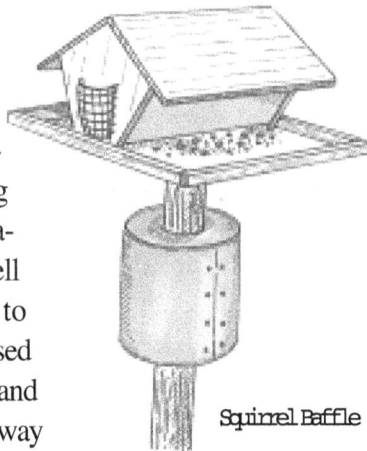

Squirrel Baffle

feeder they are doing Mach 4, and they'll usually forget to hang on. You find them under the feeder with an Excedrin® headache, planning their next attack. Sooner or later they will hang on—and everything you have is part of the fare game. Tilting baffles on the line will help discourage your squirrel from sliding down from above.

If you do not have good cover in an area you wish to place a birdfeeder, create some yourself so your birds will enjoy peace of mind. Use a four-by-four mounting post and drill several large-diameter holes into the post. In each hole place branches trimmed from trees and bushes. This will create not only cover but unlimited perching.

Ground Feeder

All it takes to make a ground birdfeeder is a little ground and a little shelter overhead. Ground feeding is a very important part of rounding out your feeding program. Many birds will eat at ground level and some even prefer it. In many cases, because birds eat in a feeding frenzy, you end up with automatic ground feeding. It is much like watching kids eating pie with no hands at the county fair—very messy. But if you plan a ground-feeding location away from the post-mounted and hanging feeders, you will be surprised at the convention of birds that will often show up there.

Seed will spoil when it gets damp or wet, so it's important that you keep ground feeders dry. A covering will help and can consist of a wooden roof system, natural brush umbrella, lean-to, or any other creative contraption that you and your birds find eye-catching.

As with any feed station, locating ground feeders near leafy, shrubby cover is very important. Too close will invite an ambush. (*Never plant ambushes in your yard.*) And just far enough away will allow for the great escape if there is a dispute over whose real estate the ground feeder is located on. I think you will be surprised at the combinations of critters who will put up with eating together if the menu is irresistible.

Eliminate Stage Fright

Hanging or post-mounted platform feeders are very popular with the birds because of the clear line of sight. Birds eat in a nervous rush because they must always look over their shoulders to see who might be sizing them up. If you decide to use a tray or platform feeder, without any covering to shed moisture, it is important that the feeder has a drain. One way would be to use screening or hardware cloth as the tray bottom. This would allow plenty of drainage and airflow through the seed. Keeping seed as dry as possible will eliminate many problems. A less-effective way to deal with moisture in platform feeders is to drill drain holes into the seed tray. With this method it is necessary to scrape and clean the tray often to remove wet and soggy seed.

Location, Location, Location

Much thought should go into the location of your birdfeeders. First, because birds are born exhibitionists, you want to be able to easily view all your little feather dusters. You also want to protect feeding songbirds from predators. Birds like to be close to thickets or shrubs that offer quick getaways. Be careful not to put the feeder so close that a cat will use it for camouflage. Height is important, not only for attracting birds but for filling the feeder. If you have several feeders put them at different heights and locations and move them around until you find the locations that attract the most attention. Just like us, birds are always looking for security. Give them a proper place to raise a family and enough to eat — in short, a good standard of living — and they'll thrive.

How many times have you gone out and stuck your birdfeeder pole in the first soft ground you could find? Or hung it on the first convenient low branch you could reach? I am amazed at how many people will spend all winter in their garages building nesting boxes and feeders that half the world's population would give anything to live in or near, and then spend two minutes placing the feeder in a location that any bird in its right mind would never be attracted to.

> *Birdseed is like manure. It's only good when you spread it around.*

A bird looks windward, so his feathers stay inward

Make sure you create some kind of windbreak for your birds and yourself near at least one birdfeeder. This gives them somewhere protected to shoot for in a blizzard or strong wind, somewhere they can comfortably find food readily available. You will also appreciate it when you head out in a blast to fill the feeder and it's so cold you have to get in the refrigerator to warm up when you return. Windbreaks will help keep your birds warm and cozy while they fill their faces. Nothing frosts a bird more than having to eat out in a cold wind. During a blizzard, tie a rope around your spouse before sending him out to fill the feeder. It is easy to get lost in a whiteout and the rope can help you find him in the spring.

Buying Seed

If you use a seed scoop, to distribute your seed to your various feeders, you will quickly figure out when you've been had. Most scoops have an opening about the size of a quarter that the seed must travel through on its way to the feeder. If your scoop continuously becomes jammed, it is quite obvious that you bought

34

more sticks and leaves than you did seed. That great price you thought you found now has to be divided by the number of pounds you have in foreign matter. Sometimes you can't see the forest for the trees, and then other times you can't see the seeds for the forest.

When you buy things in plain brown wrappers, you cannot always tell if there is truth in advertising until you get home and examine your purchase.

"Leave those big, white, dimpled ones for those stupid birds."

Most seed goes through a pretty serious culling process and is graded to regulated standards. Once you get your seed home and distributed in the yard, it goes through another culling process. This time it is looked over and picked through by every bird and furball that happens by. There have been several studies conducted on the food preferences of wild birds, but the problem is that the birds have never read them, even though they are more than willing to participate in the research. Experimenting with certain seed types to find what is most preferable will eventually save you a ton of money. There are dozens of choices, but some of the proven favorites, besides the number-one choice black-oil sunflower, are Niger thistle, white proso millet, striped sunflower, peanut parts, hulled sunflower hearts, and sunflower chips. Your hearts should go out to your birds. Sunflower and peanut hearts are favorites for many species. Which would you prefer: surf and turf or a jelly sandwich? Believe it or not, some birds go for the jelly. Try putting a small dish of grape jelly out. You will be amazed at how many birds show up to sample it.

Some birds are so eager to get to the sunflower seeds that they kick everything else out of the way, leaving much of the less-preferred seed on the ground to rot. Some will be scavenged by ground-feeding birds or squirrelly neighbors.

Because birdfeeding has become a billion-dollar-a-year industry, and everyone is trying to make a buck, many ideas have come along that birds have not bought into. One was to coat sunflower chips with soy. The black coating made the seed look like thistle, and the idea was that it could be used as a thistle substitute. My birds never touch the stuff. You can use uncoated chips as a thistle substitute and they work very well. There is no shortage of product ideas, and I urge you to experiment with cracked corn and the many mixes that are available. Keep in mind, your neighbor could be putting out the good stuff and you might end up seed-rich and bird-poor. There is nothing worse than not being able to get rid of a lot of exotic seed.

Years ago, on a plane to California, a fellow passenger told me he fed only safflower seed to his birds. He said the squirrels would not eat it and his birds loved it. You can't believe everything you hear on an airplane. Safflower seed is a noted favorite of cardinals. It would not be his first choice, but Hairy Houdini has no problem digesting safflower. If that is the only seed offered the bird variety wanes.

Nuts to Your Birds

You will find that nuts disappear quickly from your feeder if prepared and displayed properly. You will also notice a hole in your wallet. Birdseed costs peanuts, but peanuts cost money. Nutmeats are very high in protein and fat and make a great additive to any feeding program. When nuts are found in a feeder, squirrels get this glow about them. Nuts make squirrels sillier than a corn borer in a peach.

Not all birds can deal with nuts the way they are packaged by nature or man. You can't buy a can of beer nuts and put them out on the feeder along with a can opener. You also can't expect many birds to pry open shells. Some birds that are attracted to the nutmeats you offer are not equipped with the right tools to deal with the shell coverings.

Nuts can be offered in many ways. Put some out in their shells for those birds that find cracking the shells a challenge. Put others out shelled. Nut kernels will be taken by many birds and cached for later. For smaller birds, crush the nut kernels and mix them with seed.

Fruit Bar

Fruits can be a very important part of your feeding program. Fruit may be the only thing that will attract your orioles and tanagers. You can try any combination of fruit offerings in your feeding program. Most should be chopped up into tiny pieces. Apples and orange slices attract birds, but don't hesitate to try other fruit varieties. I have always had great luck feeding currants to bluebirds. I was told once that a shot glass of orange juice on my picnic table would attract orioles. They never showed up, but I did start a relationship with a cedar waxwing who didn't know when to quit.

A Hard Nut to Crack

Your birds are going to love this program. A coconut is most likely the biggest seed you will feed your birds. Just split it in half and turn in a screw eye for hanging. When you purchase the coconut, make sure it has a cut in the shell all the way around. This makes it very easy to crack open. Don't forget to drain the milk first! Coconut meat is about 60 percent fat, and your birds love fat. When they finish with the meat, you can hang the shell out like a bowl and fill it with seed. You will discover the shell is very hard when you try to put that screw eye in. If you don't want your birds to miss out on anything, give them a taste of coconut.

Put Another Log on the Wire

Using a tree branch is a cheap and easy way to build a bird-feeder. Take a two or three-inch diameter tree branch and cut it about two feet long. Drill four or five holes in it about an inch and a half in diameter. Screw an eyebolt in one end of the branch, fill the holes with a peanut butter/cornmeal mix or suet/seed mix, and hang it outside. Do not use peanut butter without mixing it with seed, cornmeal, or a similar mix. There have been reported cases of birds choking on sticky peanut butter. Many argue that this is not a problem, but why gamble? Moreover your birds will enjoy the added mix. This type of birdfeeder is very simple because you don't have to worry about perches. Those little feather dusters will hang on to the branch bark and do all kinds of acrobatics while they work away at the mix. Don't worry if they do not go to it right away; they're just barking up the wrong tree. Give them time, they'll find it.

Down on Your Fat Farm

Most people spend hours trying to get rid of excess fat, while the birds in their backyards would be more than happy to have it. One of the best things you can do for your feathered friends before you go out jogging in the morning is to make sure they have plenty of suet to munch on.

Seeds and nuts in your suet make it that much better, the way nuts and marshmallows make chocolate ice cream better. Seeds and nuts have the highest concentrations of fat and protein. Birds

38

never overeat, even though you think they might by the amount of seed they go through. It has taken them millions of years to train humans to go to the store and buy birdseed. Even when there is a very abundant food supply, you will notice that your birds eat exactly the right amount to stay lean, mean flying machines. This willpower to always eat correctly has come down through the ages of evolution. High-energy suet will have your birds pumping iron at the feeder every morning.

Let's face it, you have become attached to the baby fat that has been with you all these years. Forget losing it; just tell people you inherited the tendency to be overweight. Face the facts on your figure and figure the fats on your birds. They need a boost more than you, and suet is a great way to give it to them.

"I think those suet balls have made my face break out."

Suet recipes can be a lot of fun as long as your spouse is away for a few days. If you want your birds to stop by on a regular basis and chew the fat with you, it is important that you have suet ready and waiting when they get there. You can buy commercial suet cakes, but it isn't half as much fun or quite as messy as making your own.

> *The heaviest load you can carry is an empty birdfeeder on your conscience.*

There are many suet combinations available. There are some with peanuts, some with seed, some with fruit and berries—even a brand with fly larvae, insect eggs, and other assorted bug parts in it. I don't know how it tastes, but it smells horrible. Maybe that's why birds love it!

Do It With Suet

To make your own suet treats, start with a couple pounds of suet from your butcher. Grind two cups up real well and melt it down in a double boiler. Then let it cool until it starts to stiffen up. Then reheat the suet. I know that sounds crazy, but the reheating is supposed to harden the suet. Again, allow the suet to cool. As it starts to congeal, throw in all your goodies. You can use your imagination, but if you don't have an imagination try this: two cups of chunky peanut butter, two cups of mixed birdseed (heavy on the sunflower), and one cup of chopped nuts. If you're rich, then add two cups of chopped nuts. On top of all this you can also add a cup of the following, or a combination of all: dry dog food, cereal, cornmeal, cookies you don't want your spouse eating, or crackers.

But wait, you're not done yet. This is an all-round, super-duper suet collage. Try adding some fruit, like apples, cherries, raisins, currants, or berries. Also, crush up some eggshells and throw them in. This will give your birds a calcium boost and help digest everything else you've thrown in.

You should have everything ready to mix, because when that suet starts setting up it's not going to wait for you to go fetch the vittles.

At this point you can roll your masterpiece into eight to ten eight-ounce balls or spoon the mixture into containers. Refrigerate it until firm, or freeze it and use as needed. Freezing commercial suet blocks makes them easier to remove from containers and insert into suet cages.

Don't forget to clean the kitchen. If you memorize this recipe you're a fathead! It's almost like magic the way birds of so many varieties just seem to come out of the woodwork when you put a suet offering out for them. You see birds that have never shown themselves before and ones you never even realized lived in your vicinity. Put your suet concoction in an onion bag and hang it out where you can keep an eye on it.

Before long you will find many varieties of birds hanging from the bag upside down, right-side-up, and sideways. Certain birds can be baffled from the suet. Some suet feeder designs force the birds underneath the feeder to eat upside down. Birds that cannot cling in that position are out of luck. Starlings, for instance, will not eat fat on the bottom side of a feeder; it is beneath them. These feeders also help thwart fat little furballs. They separate the lean from the fat.

Because insect-eating birds take in a great amount of animal matter, the best substitute for this fare is ordinary beef suet. It helps them maintain their high body temperature.

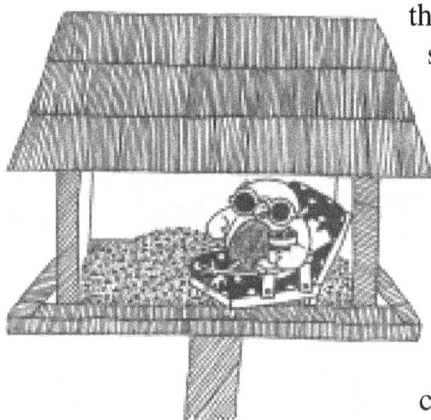

Another way to serve suet is in a basket made from wire mesh or hardware cloth. You can also buy many commercially made suet feeders.

During hot weather, suet should be put out in small portions and monitored often. Place it in a shady area to slow the spoilage.

It used to be that the butcher would give you suet for birdfeeding, but that was before birdfeeding became a big-time pastime and opened a whole new market at the meat counter. Now you can pay almost as much per pound for suet as you do for pot roast. You can usually find suet in the freezer section already wrapped in a mesh bag and ready to hang. You can always ask and maybe your butcher will even give you some for free — fat chance!

Alternative Feeding Options

Feeding dinner scraps, bread, and other baked goods to your wild birds will probably not harm them, but it will not be the most productive method of fine-tuning your feeding program. You will end up with a lot of critters you might not want to deal with.

Mealworms make great birdfeed if you can keep them in the feeder. This is not a problem during the winter in Northern states. The worms freeze up and before you know it, every chickadee in the yard is flitting around with what looks like a big fat cigar in his beak. You can get them through pet supply houses, bait shops, or mealworm distributors, (Yes, there are such businesses!) or you can grow your own.

The advantages of offering mealworms are many. They will attract insect-eating birds to the feeder; they can be refrigerated, they do not smell, and they are not slimy so handling is not a problem. They cannot escape your feeding container if they have a one-inch vertical wall retaining them, and they don't talk back.

Hummer Juice

Feeding hummingbirds is as easy as making orange juice in the morning. If you mix your own nectar, use four parts water to one part sugar. Bring to a boil to help retard fermentation. Let it cool down, then refrigerate what you don't use. Do not substitute honey for sugar. Honey can cause a fungus that has been known to affect the tiny bird's tongue. You do not want to kill your birds with kindness. Do not use additives with your homemade nectar. Adding color and sweeteners will not help attract more birds and, in some cases, can be harmful.

Do not put a lot of nectar out until you notice they're using it all. Sugar solutions are very susceptible to mold, harmful bacteria, and fermentation. Like suet, be careful to put out small amounts in shaded areas during hot weather.

Clean your hummingbird feeders regularly before each refill, using hot soapy water and a household bleach solution (one capful per gallon) or white vinegar, but rinse extremely well. If your feeder has hard-to-reach, grime-gathering grungy spots, add to the solution a dozen BBs or a handful of sand and shake, rattle, and roll. Another method used to clean feeder parts is soaking them in warm water and tossing in some denture cleaner. I guarantee it will put a smile on your hummingbird's face.

If you clean your feeder with vinegar, feel free to swig a swill yourself. It can help your arthritis, aid digestion, lower cholesterol, grow hair on your bald spots, and soothe sprained muscles from squirrel chasing.

If you are looking for a jump-start on feeding hummers, because they haven't shown up at your nectar feeder yet, try placing a flower box nearby. You don't have to go out and buy a miniature Busch Gardens; a simple flower box will get the job done. Annuals are a good choice. They are often prolific and bloom longer. You don't have to buy all red flowers; hummers like variety. Try putting some perching areas on your flower boxes. Studies show that hummers perch 60 percent of the time; they are just not noticed often in that position.

Hummingbirds weigh so little you could actually mail ten of them using a regular postage stamp. You will be surprised at how much these little egg beaters can consume. It takes a lot of energy to beat those wings as fast as they do. Their wings will go up and down 78 to 200 times per second, depending on what gear they are in. When they are in love they are in high gear.

If you watch closely, you will notice hummers do not suck the nectar from your feeder; they actually lick it out. When a hummer is thirsty, he can often get in 12 licks per second.

Now think about this: Hummers can beat their wings an average of 140 times per second, lick 12 times per second, breathe 4 times per second, and never look at the flowers they are eating from. At the same time they watch the one they plan to visit next and make sure no one else tries to beat them to it. These have to be very coordinated birds. They can fly forward, backward, upside down, and sideways. They can hover while picking and choosing which no-see-um to eat next, and then do aerial maneuvers that make the Blue Angels look like bush pilots. If you're not feeding hummers, you're missing the greatest show on Earth!

Flower Power

It's best to place your feeder near tubular flowers. These deep-throated flowers attract insects, which, along with nectar, are vital in the hummingbird diet. Hummers consume insects and derive protein from them. A bush or tree near your feeder provides welcome perching. If possible, install your feeder before insects arrive and before flowers bloom in the spring. This will give early arrivals a boost and bolster your feeding plan.

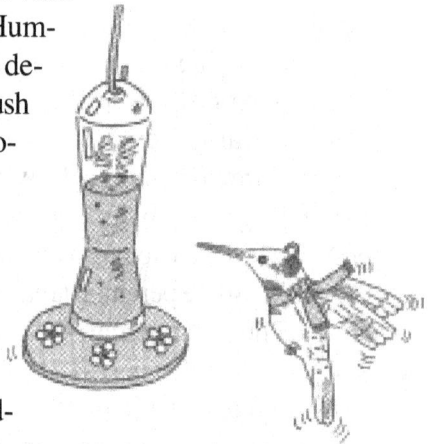

To keep ants and bees away from the hummer feeder, many people try rubbing petroleum jelly (Vaseline®) on the base of the feeder, around feeding ports, and on the hanger or post. Be careful because this can plug feeding ports. Other preventative solutions include Avon Skin-So-Soft®, but it does not last as long, and vegetable oil. There is a chance that these methods, which are not very effective, could end up contaminating the nectar offering. It is another of the many debates that have little scientific study for backup. No one has yet researched jellied birds or soft-skinned hummers.

To keep ants out of your hanging hummingbird feeder, you can also try a moat of water in the form of a little cup that hangs from a wire above the feeder. You can find them at most retail outlets that sell bird-related items.

These are not the only solutions, but you will find them much cheaper than owning an anteater. Ants are not a big problem if you change the nectar every day. You'll find that many have drowned in the solution while some are doing the backstroke. Rinse them from the feeder and refill. Often larger bird species will find the ants a great food source.

Hummingbirds are very territorial. You will notice them fighting at the feeder often. If you want to cut down on these bar brawls, place additional feeders about six feet apart and send each to his own corner.

Hummingbirds love water. They are attracted to the birdbath, but more often you will notice they're playing in the sprinkler. If you create a water mist, you will find them darting through it constantly.

Some of the most common plants that attract hummingbirds are azaleas, honeysuckle, tiger lilies, gladiolas, hollyhock, coral vine, mimosa, trumpet vine, fuchsias, and jasmine.

Do not use pesticides on flowers from which hummingbirds feed! If you are using pesticides in your yard and feeding birds, you are putting your birds at risk.

A big problem for hummingbirds is cat predation. The thought of a hummingbird hovering nearly motionless at a low bush in your yard is just too much temptation for a cat. If you put out a hummingbird feeder, be sure to locate it out of cat range. Cats can manage an easy four-to-five-foot jump if the reward is worth it. And hummingbirds are worth it.

You will also find squirrels at your hummingbird feeder occasionally. Most won't bother with it, while others are lushes for the sweet water. Most commercial feeders are pretty hard for a squirrel to grip and sip, but if yours has a sweet tooth he will find a way.

Hummer Feeder

There are many commercial hummingbird feeders available,

but if you are the crafty type you can make your own humming-bird feeders from empty salad dressing bottles. Drill a small hole in the middle of the cap, then mark the hole with a red X across the cap for the birds to target. Hang it in a harness made with bread wrapper twist ties so that the neck angles downward.

Boy Scouts in New Mexico, who built this type feeder, could approach the drinking birds and slowly move their fingers under the birds' feet until they would sit down. These birds eventually became interested in Scouting. They would hover in front of the Scouts to examine their colorful merit badges and camp patches.

Once hummingbirds begin to use a feeder on a regular basis, you can sit outside and hold the nectar feeder in your hand. Hummingbirds are not shy and will come to a hand-held feeder quickly. Hand feeding your songbirds takes a little more time and patience, but the technique is the same. You have to hold a handful of seed out until they trust you enough to perch on your palm. Before long you'll have them (and the squirrels) eating right out of your hand!

Flight Schedule

Hummingbirds, as well as other species, will leave on sched-ule no matter what you feed them or for how long.

According to most ornithologists, a hummingbird's instinctive drive to migrate is too strong to be swayed by the mere promise of food. When it's time to go, they know. Banding studies have confirmed this. Most scientists think that hummingbirds migrate in response to shorter days, not nectar feeder levels. Every year a few hummingbirds hang around too long and get caught in the deep freeze. They get confused and do not migrate for various reasons. These birds are often sick or weak or underdeveloped. Often a wildlife rehabilitator ends up with the birds and they get a free commercial flight south. If we keep doing this, soon they are all going to want a free flight. Nature would cull these birds out instead of letting them build up frequent flier miles.

As September wears on in the Northern tier states, the parade of hummers at your feeder will thin. Most likely, the last birds you see will be transients, not your regular summer visitors. After seeing no hummers for a week, take down the feeder, wash it thoroughly, and store it until spring.

Belly Up to the Bar

You can attract many types of birds to nectar feeders with larger openings and perching areas. Over sixty species will find nectar appealing. Orioles are not the only customers you will find at larger nectar feeders. In these larger containers, reduce the solution to six parts water and one part sugar.

Here is a very valuable lesson about birds: They can take you or leave you. Usually they take you, then they leave you. If you want to be taken by birds, give them some variety.

Wet and Wild

Water is one of the most important ingredients to add to a successful backyard feeding program. It is also one of the most overlooked by those trying to attract birds. A good supply of water will attract birds that do not normally come in to the feeders. Locate a water source in a shady part of your yard. This will keep the water at a cooler, more refreshing temperature in hot weather. During the winter, move it to a sunny location.

Wet birds do not fly well, so place the bath within six feet of a tree or shrub to give birds a place to fly to if the neighbor's Peeping Tom cat disturbs them while bathing.

To get birds accustomed to the bath, try placing a feed station within five feet of the bath. Birds will notice the water

as they go to the feeder. The noise of moving and splashing water fascinates and attracts birds. You can outfit the bath with a drip or mister. A mister will be attractive to hummingbirds and butterflies too!

Making a drip is a simple way of attracting birds to your water source. Even you can do it. Fill a plastic milk jug with water. Using a pin, carefully start to puncture the bottom, but do not penetrate the jug. Just make a minute hole that begins to form a drip. Hang it by its handle over the birdbath and it will drip for several hours.

Birdbath water should be changed every few days. It is also important to keep the birdbath clean. Get that vinegar out again if you haven't already used it up treating those leg cramps. Wash the bath out with water and white vinegar. The vinegar will help prevent algae growth and keep the bath fresh, but it is not as effective as a bleach solution (one capful per gallon of water) to fight birdbath algae. Be sure you rinse thoroughly and fill with clean water.

Colored aquarium gravel or marble chips, available in pet or garden centers, can be attractive in a bath and help birds get a footing. A depth of approximately two inches is ideal. Adding stones of various sizes to the birdbath will allow birds a choice of depth.

> *We never know the worth of water until the birdbath is dry.*

It is important to provide water in both summer and winter. Birds constantly tend to their feathers, which must be kept clean and healthy to ensure proper insulation and mobility, especially in winter months. Various water heaters are available to keep water from freezing in colder climates.

Keeping a water supply thawed in freezing temperatures will bring birds in close. During temperature conditions in which most natural water sources would be frozen for a long period of time, open water becomes a valuable resource. You don't have to put a heat unit in your birdbath. You can get out of your nice warm bed every morning, slip your blizzard blanket on, and take your birds some fresh water. While you're out there, fill the feeders. It is important that a bird have a bath on a regular basis. They can use snow for drinking and bathing, but a lot of snow has to be ingested to provide enough water. The amount of body heat required for a bird to melt snow puts a greater strain on metabolism and maintaining body temperature. A freeze is one of nature's ways of culling out the weak, but since man has already culled out enough birds for the next two centuries, it's time to conserve those we have left. Remember that many of the water sources they once had at their wing tips are now parking lots and fast food restaurants.

Keep Your Birds Spic and Span

If feeding stations are not kept clean, they tend to spread disease because of the unnatural congregations of birds that they attract. Droppings, mold, and spoiled feed are some of the causes and the best preventative is cleanliness. It only takes a few minutes to clean up after your birds. It is one big food fight out there all day long and things can get out of hand if you don't stay on top of it

Usually a mild solution of household bleach (one capful per gallon of water), or white vinegar and warm water and scrubbing with a bottle brush will clean a tube feeder. Caked-on debris may require soaking. Most designs come apart easily and make for easy cleanup.

The easiest feeder to maintain and keep clean is a tube feeder with a wide

49

diameter. Make sure the one you buy disassembles easily. Most have tops and bottoms that disconnect by removing clips or screws. The perch assemblies usually come apart the same way.

A brush is very handy for getting at tight spots when cleaning tube feeders. It is much harder to notice unclean conditions on wooden feed-

> *The heart fills as the birdfeeder empties.*

ers, but they too need to be cleaned and maintained as often as your other feed stations. As weird as it may sound, the easiest way to clean a birdfeeder is to take it to the car wash. I don't mean the drive-thru. Go to a do-it-yourself car wash and use a high-pressure wand with hot soapy water. You don't have to give it the hot wax. Take lots of quarters!

Crop Rotation

When you fill your feeders often, many times you are putting seed on top of seed that has been in the feeder for some time. If you top your feeder off daily, birds will never get down to this lower-level seed. So get rid of the old damp stuff. In a tube feeder, a little cat box filler or gravel in the bottom section of the tube, where the seed is seldom eaten, will help draw moisture. Fill to just below the first seed outlet. This will also cure the problems associated with small birds craning their necks into the seed outlets to snatch that last seed they see in the bottom and becoming stuck. As odd as this sounds, it happens.

Growing Wild in Your Yard

If you want to make your birds very happy, introduce some woody plant material of various heights and ground covers to provide shelter from the elements and protection from predators. Provide a variety of plant textures from feathery to prickly to offer a choice of nesting, perching, or hiding spots. Plant some ever-greens as a windbreak, and provide a steady supply of food throughout the year by selecting trees and shrubs for their fruit and seed production as well as canopy and flower color.

Use plants that are vigorous and resistant to disease and insect pests. This will help you abstain from using pesticides, which will defeat the whole purpose behind your efforts to attract wildlife to your yard. Again, you have a responsibility to protect those animals you invite into your yard. If you have had a checkered past of chemical dependency, it is not too late to "Just Say No" to pesticides.

Shrubs and trees vary geographically, so few general suggestions can be made. The most popular shrub and tree fruits are mulberry, blackberry, rose, mountain ash, cherry, elderberry, serviceberry, sumac, holly, grape, and dogwood. Your best information will come from a knowledgeable local nursery owner or state and local agricultural offices. Many states have nongame wildlife divisions with plenty of free materials to share with citizens interested in attracting wildlife to their property by planting native plants. There are also books available on this subject. A little research on your part will lead you to a wealth of good reliable information. Planning is half the fun. Plants take a long time to grow, so do it right the first time!

> *Never judge a bird by its cover.*

Bird Plantings

When you plant your garden this spring, let the birds help you. Instead of putting a fence around your flower garden, zigzag it through the garden. Put a couple strands of cord or wire from post to post so that the birds can sit and sow. They will deposit a wide variety of prefertilized seeds. As these plants bloom, you will learn what your birds like to dine on. If it attracted them once, it surely will attract them again. Bird planting works. We have a beautiful planet to prove it.

Weed your garden. Don't take them out; put them in. Birds love weed seeds. Thistle, dandelion, chickweed, knotweed, and

51

more. Whether you summer in the country or simmer in the city, you too can have a weed garden.

When planting to attract birds, remember to consider plant species that will offer food choices, act as nesting habitat, and offer shelter from weather and predators. No matter how small an area you have to work with, a plan can be devised to include several different habitats that will offer the important needs that birds require.

Lawn Ranger

Anyone can argue that their lawn is not that big, so those little cans of weed killer and bug spray are not a problem. Now consider that there are approximately 100 million lawns in North America covering 40 to 50 million acres.

Lawns are nothing new. The Chinese grew them five thousand years ago. What is new are the many chemicals they are treated with. The lawn was a status symbol in Colonial America, just as it had been in Europe. In 1841 the lawn mower was introduced. It replaced the lawn *moo*er. One professor who has studied such phenomena thinks lawn preference is genetically encoded in man because at one time we were foragers in the grasslands of the world. Another theory is that lawns are a way of taming and domesticating nature. Another explanation makes lawns a mapping device, a way of marking one's territory. Animals have many ways of marking their territory; man seems to prefer defending his with poison.

When you think about it, lawns are monumental wastes of time, money, and ecological resources. Let them grow wild. Start a prairie grass movement in your neighborhood. Each year you can get together with the neighbors and have a prairie fire. This will help keep your prairie grasses healthy. It will also bring the urban buffalo population back to your neighborhood, and your birds will go wild over all the natural food sources you will be providing.

Roosting Box

Generally, birds roost in the same habitat they nest in. That means if you plant good nesting habitat, you also create good roosting habitat. A dense stand of evergreens, in cold regions of the country, are very actively used for roosting, not only when the north wind blows but year-round.

Many birds will use roosting boxes when the weather quickly turns. These structures are simply wooden windbreaks with a series of perches to accommodate a number of birds. Often birds will crowd into empty nesting boxes during severe weather.

Customer ID

I know the face, I just can't place the name. Identifying birds at the feeder is usually a very simple process of elimination. Instead of buying a field guide that lists every bird on the globe, start out with a local field guide for your specific geographical area. These guides are readily available. They usually list approximately 100 species, which makes the process of discovering who your guests are much easier. The first group you will notice are your regulars. These are permanent resident birds that will stick with you through thick and thin, rain and wind.

Once you have become acquainted with the regulars, it will make it that much easier to figure out who the migrants are. Remember, males and females do not always look alike. A common mistake in identifying birds is not knowing what the female of a species looks like. Novice bird-watchers tend to key in to the colorful males first.

A song in your heart is great, but etching bird-songs and calls

in your brain is a better way of knowing what birds are in the area. If you watch birds long enough at the feeders, you will begin to notice not only what they prefer to feed on and what sounds they emit but also their habits and personal quirks, their postures, flight patterns, personal hygiene, the birds they hang out with, and the birds that intimidate them.

Absence Makes Your Birds Go Yonder!

One more reminder before we move on—if you are a traditional "winter-only" feeder of birds, do not stop feeding in the spring until new natural growth and awakening critters begin to generate a fresh food supply. Spring is the most critical time for birds. They have used up much of winter's stores. Spring weather is unpredictable. Competition is stiff, as migrants return and many people who are not as smart as you stop feeding too early. If you are going away for an extended period of time, your birds will be fine. However, it would only be polite to wean them off your seed offerings before you leave. They are able to survive a cold-turkey stoppage of seed, but they will always hold a grudge. You create a void in your birds' lives when you're absent. They start feeling lonely and hungry—especially hungry. You run the risk of leaving emotional scars on your birds if you just leave without taking their feed and feelings into consideration. The bulk of their diet is from natural food sources, but shutting off a dependable seed flow in harsh weather conditions could put your birds in a bind.

Recap and Reinforce

• Regardless of the season, seed that spends any amount of time on the ground is exposed to contamination by bacteria, animal droppings and dampness.

• Seed trays with drainage holes will quickly clog with wet seed, droppings and hulls. Screening works much more efficiently.

• Diseases like salmonella can be spread through feed stations, growing in moldy, damp seed, and bird droppings, left by the many visitors to the feeder. Clean birdfeeding accessories often in a tub of hot, soapy water and disinfectant.

• Use a small-capacity hummingbird nectar feeder and exchange sugar water often unless you have so many hummers you need a full-time air traffic controller.

• Separate seed types into various feeders. This will help reduce the wasted seed caused by picky-pecky birds throwing out seed that does not appeal to them, looking for the morsels that do. It is often worse than a kid going through the Cracker Jack box looking for the prize.

• Using a suet feeder that only allows access from the bottom will limit clientele. Starlings have been known to use these feeders but find it downright rude to have to perch upside-down.
• If you fill a five-pound-capacity birdfeeder with six-pounds of seed, you must hold your breath while pouring the last pound and let it slowly mound up as you pull the scoop slowly upward and away from the feeder hopper.

• If your neighbor has seven feeders, you should multiply this number by two and add more overall capacity to gain back the birds you lost to his aggressive feeding technique.

• Birds do not sweat. It is not known whether they have no sweat glands because they do not sweat, or they do not sweat because they have no sweat glands.

• Many birds shut their wings periodically while flying to conserve energy and open them again to prevent crash landings.

Dear Dick E. Bird

Dear Dick E. Bird:

My neighbor comes for coffee a few times a week. We sit and watch the birds at the feeder while we chat. She mentioned that bringing birds into one spot is just a sure way to spread diseases. She has never fed them for this reason. Do you think I should stop? —Mary Ellen in Palos Heights

Dear Mary Ellen:

Yes, I think you should stop seeing your neighbor. If she has never fed birds, how did she become such an expert on avian disease? Maybe she is just too cheap to spring for a little seed. It is healthy to have this fear of filth. Clean feeders often and put out a few more so your birds do not congregate in one eatery. I don't want you to become known as Typhoid Mary Ellen. A little sanitary concern will keep your birds healthy, stealthy, and wise.

—Keep Smilin', Dick E. Bird

Dear Dick E. Bird:

My husband says mowing the lawn disturbs the birds, and if you do it on a regular basis they will leave and not come back. He says they are very sensitive to noise pollution and they find lawn mower sound very offensive. I have spent a lot of time welcoming birds to my yard and garden, and I would hate to jeopardize my relationship with them. My husband never seemed that concerned about the birds before. What do you think?

—Knee High in Bloomingdale

Dear Knee High:

I think you should buy your husband a push mower. That would kill two birds with one stone (so to speak).

—Keep Smilin', Dick E. Bird

Tongue-in-Beak Tidbits

If you think you have digested this material, move on to the next chapter. If not, don't feel bad, some people are just naturally slow!

APPLY FEATHERED FACTS

1. What seed do 80 percent of songbirds prefer?
2. What should you look for when buying a one-ton capacity birdfeeder?
3. What are the two most important characteristics to look for when buying a birdfeeder?
4. Is there any such thing as a squirrel-proof birdfeeder?

DISCUSSION TOPICS

1. Should you feed hummingbirds honey?
2. What is the best way to attract birds without using feeders?
3. In birdfeeding what does the term "supply and demand" mean?
4. What can birds eat when snow covers the ground?

BIRD BRAINED TRIVIA

1. What percentage of the world's birds migrate?
2. Why do birds throw back their heads when drinking?
3. Do birds drink and bathe in the same water?
4. What weighs more, a pound of sunflower seed or a pound of thistle seed?
5. What is it called when birds eat too much ripe fruit and become intoxicated?

AND THE ANSWER IS—

Apply Feathered Facts: 1. Black-oil sunflower. 2. A psychiatrist. 3. Seed visibility and easy cleaning. 4. Only for stupid squirrels. **Discussion Topics:** 1. Never give them honey, honey! It ferments quickly and can result in a tongue fungus. 2. Planting cover and food-producing vegetation, and establishing a water source. 3. You're supplying the seed your birds demand. 4. Insects in the bark of trees and soft parts of seed. **Bird-Brained Trivia:** 1. 20 percent. 2. Only a few birds drink by suction. All other birds take the water into their mouths and throw their heads back in order to swallow. 3. Yes, and not necessarily in that order. 4. A pound is a pound the world around—unless it's a kilogram. 5. The Wrath of Grapes.

The graceful bird, oh, what is faster.
Till it hits the window, oh, what a disaster.
The door to success is hard to attain,
For the window of opportunity comes with a pane.
                                          —Dick E. Bird

3•

Birdfeeding's Little Aggravations

Shoot the Neighbor, Not the Cat!

If you have a problem with a neighbor's cat eating your birds, don't get rid of the cat—get rid of the neighbor, because the neighbor will just buy another cat. Studies have shown that at least 16 million songbirds and 140,000 game birds are killed annually by domestic cats. The Humane Society estimates that 35,000 kittens are born every day in the United States alone. One female cat and her cute litter of kittens can produce over 400,000 cats in just seven years!

A big step toward control would be to promote spaying and neutering. Some ordinances require cat owners to purchase licenses. The fees are much lower for spayed and neutered cats, just as they currently are for dogs. This action would not only help save millions of birds every year, but would also help to reduce the number of cats that have to be destroyed.

Cats come in all sizes and varieties. They are all great bird-watchers. Hunting and stalking are instinctive to them, and over half the cats in North America are strays.

Livetrapping wild domestic cats is very easy if you have a good commercial trap. These cat traps are available at most hardware stores and also work for squirrel relocation. You can then deposit the cats at your local humane society. Until communities begin establishing leash laws for cats, the same way we do for dogs, cats will continue to multiply out of control and greatly impact our wild bird populations.

Catastrophe

If you don't think your cat could ever catch a bird, consider some of their abilities. They see very well in the dark. Their eyes are light reflectors, almost completely covered by the pupil. During the day, the pupils narrow to slits, but in the dark they are wide open, kind of a "cat scan." Cats have radar ears and sonar noses. The whiskers on a cat's face are very important. (This is why cats never shave.) The twenty or so hairs on the cat's face are all tied to sensitive nerves that supply information to the brain, which is on full alert.

The argument that cats pose no more threat than birds of prey is built on a weak premise. Cats are unnatural predators. Unlike natural predators such as the fox and the raccoon, the cat is often well-fed and in good health, making them unnaturally efficient.

Parental Guidance

Please let me clarify my position. I am not picking on cats. I am picking on cat owners. I have cats myself. They never go outside because if they did, they would kill birds. If you feed birds and let your cat run loose, you are simply feeding your birds to your cat. I have heard all the excuses: "I feed tabby high-quality cat food, so she is never hungry" or "My cat is declawed" or "My cat is too old to catch birds" or "I never let my cat out at night." None of these excuses add up to common sense. The truth is, cats have always preyed on birds—period.

Cats sleep over half their lives away. The other half, I can guarantee you, they are stalking. (They probably even stalk in their sleep.)

"This time I'll peck on his head and you bite his tail!"

At the National Audubon Society's annual conference in 1905, cats were targeted as the biggest reason for songbird population declines. At that time the Society stated: "In the interest of humanity and bird protection, the National Audubon Society endorses the movement to make owners responsible for their [cats'] acts and welfare." (Even back then it was calculated that millions of birds were killed each year.)

Bird and cat relationships are illegal, immoral, and fattening. Cats move through the dark without making a sound, checking every nook and cranny in their domain. A cat can move with such lightning quickness and the accuracy of a heat-seeking missile that the victim often never knows what hit him. So keep tabs on your tabbies!

Hawking Your Birds

As more and more birds are finding pleasure in the many and varied birdfeeder offerings, hawks, cats, squirrels, and assorted nocturnal, hairy wildlife are drawn to the crowd that your seed attracts.

One sight most everyone witnesses around the feeder sooner or later is the sharp-shinned hawk. Small birds are a big part of a hawk's diet. It is very natural for these and other species of hawks to hunt birds, so don't get too upset. If they aren't eating your birds, they will be eating someone else's. It is not a good idea to make easy pickings of your birds. If you find a hawk monitoring your feeder on a regular basis, shut your feed stations down for a while. The hawk will move on to more productive feather foraging in a different setting. Blue jays might squawk a lot, but they are one of nature's most efficient alarm systems. When predators come into an area, the jay is the first to announce their arrival.

> **Birds that prey together stay together.**

Sharpies are very adept at moving through ground-level tangles in the pursuit of happiness. To them happiness comes in many shapes, sizes, and colors that are most likely hovering around your feeder. Sharpies are not large, but these birds are awesome aerial hunters. As they speed in on their prey, they extend their long legs forward and lock in on their target.

Some experts say it is not even necessary to shut down your feed stations if a hawk zeroes in on your dependents. Studies have shown that these party crashers only thin out the slow, stu-

63

pid, weak, young, and diseased birds. Supposedly, the stronger, smarter birds survive.

That's just great unless you're a slow, stupid bird. Some researchers insist that bird populations are affected by food supply and nesting habitat and that predation just doesn't matter.

So stop worrying about hawks cruising your cuisine — that's what they do for a living.

"Do I have Prudential? Yes, why do you ask?

Life Is Full of Hard Knocks

Spring is usually the heavy casualty season at the feeder and window panes. The nesting season is always a feverish time of activity, and the results of trying to fit courtship, nest building, feeding, and flight lessons, all into such a short period of time, create many accidents.

During the nesting season, many young birds are found outside the nest. In most cases, this is very normal. They may or may not need your help. In 90 percent of the situations they do not. They are about to fly and are still under the care of their parents. If you want to do something worthwhile, just watch this process and keep an eye out for any marauding cats.

Although it is illegal by federal and state law to keep wild birds in captivity without a permit, many birds are spared each year by good Samaritans who find them in need of a little loving care.

Often birds will die from shock. Shock can be caused not only from slamming headlong into a picture window, but also from something as common as fear. Many times a bird that has been ruffled by a cat, but is otherwise uninjured, will still die from shock.

A bird that cannot use its legs, or seems weak and lethargic

64

and will not eat, is usually a victim of poisoning. Those pesticides you use around the house can sometimes end up in your birds because they eat the bugs and the weed seeds you are trying to treat. Statistics show that it only takes a dozen or so poisoned earthworms to kill a robin and less for their young. Is a green lawn worth a silent yard? Pesticides kill by attacking the nervous system. The effect of the poison intensifies and the bird slowly dies.

I had a bird at the feeder one day with a toothpick taped to his leg. Evidently, someone had set his leg. I don't know if he had an appointment to go back and get it removed or not. At least he will never have a problem cleaning his teeth. Common sense is the best method of handling bird encounters. So if you have any, use that first. If you know a bird in serious trouble, call a local wildlife rehabilitator.

Clearly a Pane in the Neck

Birds running into your windows is a constant problem, and if the yearly total of birds lost to this situation were known accurately it would be very depressing. There are many things that can be done, but none is foolproof. You will always have some fool fly right into one again. The more common methods of marking the windows are with sun-catchers, hawk silhouettes, or colored streamers. Many people put up a trellis so that birds think about a partial barrier before they even get to the window. Shades can be closed to cut the window glare and, if all else fails, use netting to catch those feather brains before they hit the hard stuff.

After all this, it makes you wonder why you ever put a window there in the first place. You can't see much through a shaded, netted, streamer-clad window with hawk silhouettes stuck all over it, can you?

Putting the feeders up close to the window may be of some help. It gives birds less acceleration from the time they leave the feeder and hit the window. By doing this, you get an extremely close look at your customers, and they realize there is a window close by because they can see your nose stuck to it.

You might also want to try a window box. Make it big enough to provide a little water and a few plants to attract hummers and stick a couple suction-cupped window feeders just above it all. This still leaves you the view you had in mind when you installed the window in the first place and, hopefully, enough activity around it to keep songbirds from trying to fly through it.

Crash Dummy

I ran to the window, I heard a thud.
There lay a bird facedown in the mud.
He looked of a sailor, on shore leave from duty.
Eyes were all glassy and expression was fruity.
I said, "Com'on, matey, I'll give ye a hand."
And tried to see if the poor bird could stand.
He wobbled and staggered and jostled his head,
At one point I looked and thought he was dead.
But soon he was breathing and trying to squawk.
So I leaned him to starboard to see if he'd walk.
He didn't do much, his mind came and went,
And when he took off, there wasn't a hint.
He burst for the air and went for a tree,
Like a sobering sailor headed for sea.   —DICK E. BIRD

A cheaper method of silhouetting your windows, when birds are flocking to them, would be to use window cleaner to "flock" your windows. My grandmother's cousin, while lying in bed dying of cancer, entered a slogan contest for a cleaning product that is still used today. The product was a powdered cleaner called Bon Ami®, the logo is a chick, and the slogan she wrote is "Hasn't scratched yet!" Youngsters often use this product to "flock" or

66

"ice" windows with snowflake templates during the Christmas holidays. The cleaner is made into a paste and dabbed on with a sponge and dries a powdery white. You can use this same method to dab a few silhouettes on your problem windows.

Another product to use for this method is Glass Wax®. You can add food coloring if you desire a colorful silhouette when the liquid dries. Both products can be wiped off at any time and they clean your windows to boot!

If you decide to go with the silhouette method, or a picture of your mother-in-law, you can find them at your local bird store or cut your own out of vinyl or cardboard. And don't forget, it always helps to keep your windows dirty!

911

When you hear a window strike, go out right away and see if you can find a casualty. Often the crash is minor and just gets the bird's attention. If you do find a bird below the window, make sure the head is back and the airway open. In most cases you will find the bird in either a state of shock or dead from a severe concussion. Seldom do they break their necks or the window. If the bird is still alive, it will have the symptoms of a closed head injury. The talons or claws will be curled up as if the bird has had a stroke. Take the bird and place it in a box. Put the box in a dark quiet area. If the bird is going to survive, it will most likely come around and be ready for release in a couple hours. If the bird has broken its wing, you will have to contact a wildlife rehabber to care for it. Larger birds that hit your windows are usu-

"Try to find a lawyer that will work for bird scratch!"

ally hawks tailgating a songbird. They will show the same symptoms and can be treated the same way. The recovery time is usually twice that of a songbird. I have had hawks go four and five hours before they are ready to sit up like drunken sailors with glassy eyes and think about liftoff. Watch the talons. They can spoil your whole day. Most birds do not realize you are trying to help them. The less they see you the better off they will be. Nothing personal, but your face can scare a bird to death. The reason for the dark quiet box is so the bird can rest and not have to deal with the added trauma of looking at you.

The Hoarding Hoover Birds

Jays, also known as the vacuum cleaners of the birdfeeding world, are really not the hoarding varmints they are made out to be. Think of them more as your UPS driver. They simply pick up your seed and distribute it to others. They are actually hiding it for themselves, but there are no secrets in the woods and fields — and many eyes. If you watch, you can witness small songbirds raiding the jay's cache seconds after he departs.

For various reasons, you will come to despise some of the birds that show up at your feeder. In most cases you will never make your feed station species-specific, but you can work toward that end. Knowing the enemy is the first rule of combat. You spend time and money making things perfect for the birds you hope to attract — so just reverse this thinking. Study the birds you wish to exclude. Make things as miserable as you can for the birds you would rather see perched at your neighbor's house.

Find out what they prefer in cuisine and take it off the menu. Find out what type of seating arrangements they enjoy and remove them. Most people, it seems, want to eliminate most birds that prefer ground and platform feeders. So just give those feeders to your neighbor. Selective feeding will help you tune out birds that do not fit into your adoption plan.

Darling Starlings

From their entry point in New York City, Sturnus vulgaris, better known as the vulgar starlings, began colonizing North America over one hundred years ago. Ornithologists all agree that it was New York where the birds developed their pushy attitude. From there the birds made their way across North America very quickly. Their success was fueled by a desire to go west and explore the vast new land that extended over each horizon and their aggressive personality, which many native birds have learned to detest.

Today it is estimated that over 120 million starlings inhabit North America. These birds obnoxiously take habitat away from native birds and have especially been damaging to our bluebird populations. But they are not the only species that has caused problems to native birds. The English sparrow also steals valuable habitat from native species. The worst offender, with exactly the same growth and direction pattern, but much more destructive to native habitat, is the odd duck who lives within all of us!

Knock It Off

If woodpeckers are eating your house, it could mean one of several things: Your woodpecker could be in love and building a nesting cavity in the side of your house, or he could be looking for bugs, or he could just be drumming to other woodpeckers—you know—making house calls! It also usually means you are going to get new siding.

One woodpecker theory is that the smaller birds, like the brown creepers, feed at your suet then walk up and down the side of your house with grease on their feet. This grease wipes off on the house and attracts insects. The insects attract the woodpecker and soon your house looks like Swiss cheese.

Usually one hole means a nesting cavity. One or two small holes means the bird is marking its territory. A whole line of small holes means your house is bugged. Big holes that you can drive your car through usually mean pileated woodpeckers.

Woodpeckers Do Not Get Headaches

Unlike us, these birds do not get migraines from beating their heads against the wall. Although there are many different types of woodpeckers, all of which differ anatomically, woodpeckers have one common denominator: thick skulls. They are very hardheaded birds. All woodpeckers are frequent fliers, but some more than others are persistent peckers. Members of those species are designed with special advantages. Their skulls are curved inward at the upper bases of the bills so that the skulls are not attached to their bills. The reason most of us have headaches is because we cannot detach ourselves from our bills, as these birds do.

"I think they are marking our territory now, Ernie."

This advanced avian engineering acts like a shock absorber and allows these birds to save face. Woodpecker bills can take a beating and go on feeding. They look fragile, but the tips are narrow and extend to broad bases that are remarkably sturdy. These little chiselers not only are protected from sudden-impact headaches, but also those caused from inhaling environmentally unsafe air. In the birdhouse industry, we call this "sucking sawdust."

Woodpeckers' nostrils are narrow slits that keep wood chips from flying up into their noses and causing sinus headaches, which are the worst types for woodpeckers to shake. Wood chips they

70

produce are chunky, not long and narrow, so an average chip will not fit up a woodpecker's nose.

Woodpeckers are protected under the Migratory Bird Act. Of all the scare tactics I have used to rid my house of woodpeckers, I find harassment the best deterrent. It is important to understand that harming wildlife is not an answer, it is just another problem. Chasing woodpeckers away with a light spray of water from the garden hose has proven effective for some. The birds quickly decide the area is not safe and go directly to your neighbor's house. Your siding can also take abuse from squirrels climbing over it to reach a feeder near the house. Moving the feeder or growing some vines are two ways of dealing with traction marks on the side of your house.

Filling and Spilling

Filling your feeder can often be a mess. If the opening is not wide, you can end up having more seed on the ground than in the feeder. There are commercial scoops, but why spend the money when you have a great scoop right in the refrigerator? A simple way to fill your birdfeeders is with a plastic gallon milk jug. Simply take the jug and cut the bottom off at a slight angle (drink the milk first). You now have a scoop. When you are ready to fill, just screw off the cap and slip the spout in your feeder opening. Put the whole thing in—Lark, Stork, and Barrel—then run for the house. Do this every half hour as the feeder empties.

Fill several empty milk jugs with your favorite seed and have them ready for action when the feeder hits bottom. Your birds are not accustomed to waiting for some uncoordinated, two-legged seed hauler with a slow shovel.

Due-Due Economics

Seed prices go up and down because of supply and demand. Increasing prices are often due to the effects of a weaker dollar

71

and not to the enthusiasm created by an ever-increasing number of people feeding birds. After you eat breakfast and put enough gas in your car to get to the feed store, there often isn't enough of your dollar left to buy any birdseed no matter what the price.

Birds, ya know, don't got no bladder,
So wherever they is, it just don't matter.
On the deck or on the sills,
The spirit moves, you hear a trill.
Then they fly, just like a thief,
That is how they spell relief.
　　　　　—DICK E. BIRD

Do not be alarmed that a huge portion of your seed income is turned into fertilizer. It is not the end result that you should be concerned with. Bread is cheap, but it has little or no nutritional value for your birds, and that is why you should spring for the good stuff. You can't take your money with you, but by turning it into bird droppings, you are probably as close to it as you can get.

> *Birds of a feather flock to a newly washed car.*

Bird droppings can be annoying. They often give a house a nautical flavor by turning the back porch into a poop deck. It is important to understand avian waste composition. If you have ever done any long-distance driving, you might have had hours to study bird droppings on your windshield and ponder life's important questions, like "What is the black dot in the center of an otherwise white bird dropping?" It is actually nature's way of camouflaging avian waste to protect it from scat collectors. The answer is as simple as No. 1 and No. 2. The black dot in the center is fecal matter. The white blanketing matter is urine. These two substances are really one and are voided and avoided in concert and at concerts. The black dot of feces spins directly in the middle of the droppings because the urine has a gravitational force field. Both types of matter become separated and break down quickly when agitated by window washer and wiper action simultaneously.

Washtub Rowdies

A robin with an attitude can splash all the water out of the birdbath in two minutes. Usually birds will take turns at the bath, but like the feeder, there is a seniority roster and this will sometimes create confusion. Most birds will follow the pool rules and sit facing the water. But there will always be birds that perch to a different drum. Some birds insist on perching at the birdbath bass-ackwards. The reason birds do this occasionally is to cool their heels before they wet their whistles. Birds will use a bath for several reasons. Drinking is one, bathing another, also preening and cooling. Then there's one that most people never think about—reflec-

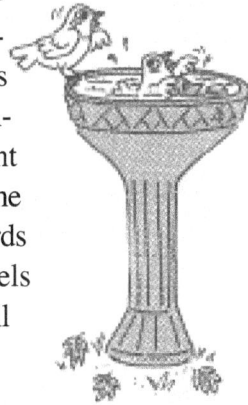

"Hey, I said I wanted a drink first!"

tion. Many birds will sit on the side of the bath in shallow thought, just staring at their own reflections. Some birds have a hard time facing the everyday realities of raising their young, working on spousal relationships, and earning a living. They often cannot face themselves, so they sit bass-ackwards on the edge of the birdbath with their tails dragging.

> *A goose in the birdbath is just good clean fun.*

Head Banging

If you have a bird banging his head against your window, pecking your pane, and kung-fu kicking your hubcaps, do not be upset. He is not trying to tell you the birdfeeder is empty. He is fighting mad—but not at you. He is actually mad at himself. Especially in the spring, birds become very territorial and once they stake out some turf and start looking for a little romance, they do not want any competition trying to elbow in on the action. The reason these birds are fighting mad is that they see themselves in the window reflection and think it is another bird as good-looking as themselves. They will sit there and do bird-battle with their reflection for days unless you break it up.

The quickest way to deal with this problem is to block the reflection. If a bird can't see himself, he will think he won and go off with his chest all puffed out. If you don't do something, he will, in all likelihood, beat himself to death. Birds have been observed doing this against all kinds of reflective objects.

Overexertion

Some people have given up birdfeeding because it was too much exercise but an often-overlooked benefit of backyard birdfeeding is the weight loss factor. Research now proves that maintaining an extensive birdfeeding program can mean beneficial burn-off of unwanted calories. Here are just a few statistical examples:

Filling the Feeder with Ten Pounds of Seed
If feeder is within reach .... 25 calories
If feeder is twenty feet off the ground .... 75 calories
Hand-to-hand combat with a squirrel........1,250 calories

Going to Town for Birdseed
If the feed store owner loads it for you .... 2 calories
If your spouse loads it while you supervise .... 5 calories
If you load it while your spouse nags .... 900 calories
If you fight over the price .... 1,200 calories
If you lose the fight........................... 1,550 calories

Night Feeding

Unless you take your birdfeeders down every night when you go out to get the flag, you are already a night feeder, but most people only see the aftermath in the morning. So why not stay up a little later, put a light on the feed station, and watch the show?

Critters coming in at night and raiding birdfeeders can be a nuisance, but if you are a night owl, late-night feeding can be very enjoyable. You won't find birds at the feeder, but there are numerous other creatures that enjoy night feeding using the Braill method. Flying squirrels, raccoons, opossums, deer, bear, porcupines, and skunks will be the most common clientele coming in for a midnight snack. One method of controlling the mess they make is offering them their own feeder. A clean paint roller pan is an excellent choice. You throw some seed in the pan and attach it to a deck or railing.

The larger raccoon and opossum will spend their time eating from this easy-access feed tray, and the bulk of the droppings all end up in the pan. In the morning the pan is easily washed out and put away.

Rodent Rip-Off

Ground squirrels will hang out around the base of the birdfeeder like teenagers at the mall. They look like they are loitering, but they're actually there for a purpose. Ground squirrels are very hardworking tunnel rats. They will build miles of tunnels under the foundation of your house and help you settle down. They collect the birdseed those ungrateful birds have scattered all over the ground and store it in underground vaults. In the fall they fatten up on seed, insects, and grass before taking a little nap (for about six months). The seed these little janitors collect often ends up in a bird because ground squirrels are common hawk bait.

There Are No Guarantees in Life

Ants can cause many headaches for your bird-attracting efforts. There are dozens of remedies. I have tried many and found none to be foolproof. Some people have tried cinnamon around the post that holds the hummingbird feeder; others claim ants will not tolerate vinegar. You can use water to baffle ants before they reach the feeder. Create a moat of water by using a small funnel placed upside down on a wire and puttied into place.

Ants are not a real problem if you change the nectar every day. I have watched birds chowing down on ant-covered fruit halves. Hanging fruit will partially solve ant-attraction problems. Some ants get nosebleeds when they climb too high.

In the South, fire ants can be a real nuisance in nesting boxes and around feeders. I have had plenty of experience with fire ants. I am still not convinced they are not aliens. I once read a study from the University of Florida that recommended using boiling water on fire ant mounds. The theory was that chemical warfare just made the ants disperse and form new colonies. They reacted to the water as a natural event and held their ground. Repeated applications of boiling water on mounds reduce ant colony numbers drastically and are a good way to keep the little pests in check.

Birdfeed earwigs

Birds are not the only winged creatures you will find at the feeder. There could come a time when you go out to the birdfeeder, pop the top, and find little critters that look mean at both ends, crawling through the canyons and crevices of your seed dispenser. These are earwigs. They love moist living spaces. The name "earwig" comes from a time when wigs were fashionable. Fashion is a cyclical process. For a while it's short hair, then long hair, purple hair, no hair, and fake hair. When our forefathers were wearing fake hair, these flying insects were attracted to the sweaty hairpieces. It was believed at the time that these bugs would sometimes climb into the ear canal and bore right into the brain of the wig wearer, causing insanity or sometimes insect starvation. So if you think birdfeeding is driving you — or someone you love — crazy, have your ear wigs checked and clean your birdfeeders more often. Moist cardboard will attract earwigs, which can then be easily disposed of.

Handy Birds

On damp and snowy mornings, many people wind up falling head over heels for their birds while filling the feeders. Feeding wild birds creates hazards, but along with each come many rewards. One such reward is handfeeding some of your regular customers. Mastering handfeeding is a simple three-step procedure. Step No. 1: Stand statue-still, do not turn your head, and do not blink. Step No. 2: Do not swallow, lick your lips, or scratch any part of your body. Step No. 3: Hold your hand out away from your body and do not breathe.

Birds will begin checking you out and doing "touch-and-go's" off your longest fingers. Soon they will snatch a seed, and eventually they will sit a spell. Once they have relaxed enough to sit on your hand, you can breathe easy.

But be careful. These new friends can sometimes become a nuisance. I had a pet starling once that would land on any head that happened into the yard. This sent many friends into shock and was often annoying. My wife was visiting the hairdresser one day when he remarked, "Have you been painting?" My wife said, "No, why do you ask?" Our starling had made a deposit on one of his visits.

The secrets to building a relationship with your birds are trust, consistency, and caring. To handfeed, be patient and let birds become used to your presence and your offering. To quicken the process, you can eliminate their other seed choices while you are out trying to train them. Expect a chickadee long before you have a buzzard eating out of your hand—unless you forget to breathe.

Gandering Geese

Canada geese have been taking a lot of flak lately, some of it from the muzzles of shotguns. Utopia to a goose is a manicured lawn, ponds, and a free lunch. They have found this combination at golf courses, housing developments, and on the grounds of large commercial buildings that have their own water-treatment facilities. The increasing populations of Canada geese come from stress-free (no predators) living. Until they became a nuisance,

Canada geese were cute and people fed them regularly. They formed flocks of non-migrating beggars with an enormous capacity to produce fertilizer.

Some municipalities have found it necessary to permit special hunting in city parks. Others trap and relocate the geese, rope off areas with reflective tape, and introduce mute swans that harass the birds and drive them away.

One town in Wisconsin live-trapped their problem geese and under the cloak of night trucked them to a nearby town across the border in Minnesota. They were caught in the act, and the geese were back in Wisconsin before the goose transporters were through explaining themselves to Minnesota authorities.

Bug Your Birds

One sure way to monitor the activity in your feeding area is to wire it for sound. There are electronic products, found at wild birdfeeding stores, designed to filter out background noise and tune in to birds. A wireless monitor, attached to your feeder, will send bird audio into your house. I use one of these devices just so I know when my dog is drinking out of my birdbath. My birds do not slurp as much as my dog, so it's a sure giveaway when I hear slurping broadcast into the house!

I still think these devices should be a two-way system, making it convenient to yell at squirrels. These products do help in learning birdsongs and calls, and at the same time alert listeners to interesting activities in the yard they may want to witness.

Recap and Reinforce

• A woodpecker busting bugs on your house uses a very powerful tool. His beak hits your siding at a velocity of 1,300 miles per hour. This means that when the head snaps back, the brain is subject to a deceleration of about 1,000 G's.

• Cats and birds mix about as well as oil and water. If you have cats and feed birds, you must take extreme precautions. Keeping the cat indoors is really the only option because it is much easier keeping the birds outdoors. Anyone who thinks his cats do not bother the birds is a fool. This simply means he is trying to fool you or has already fooled himself. Cats are born with birds on the brain. You can't break a cat (of chasing birds), so don't even try. Keep 'em home, don't let 'em roam; heed my words, or else they'll get your birds!

• Bees will often visit birdfeeders in the early spring, attracted by pollen that has accumulated on the seed.

• If you find young birds that have fallen out of the nest it is most often best to leave them alone. Very young birds can be picked up and put back in the nest. The adults will not reject nestlings that have been handled. That is a myth most people perpetuate for some reason. Most birds smell bad, meaning they don't smell good. I guess what I am trying to say is: Most birds have a poor sense of smell, so they won't know you have been fooling with their kids while they were out.

• When an object's lift is greater than its weight, it will rise into the air. And when thrust is greater than drag, that object will move in the direction of the thrust force. These principles explain why and how a bird lifts and thrusts and drags his weight back and forth to the birdfeeder until his cargo outweighs his capacity to thrust his lift and drag his waist until the waste is thrust and, again, lift allows drag.

• Bird droppings are acidic. Because of this, new cars have been designed to depreciate very quickly. Long before the corrosive effects of bird droppings can ruin your paint job, the car probably won't be running any longer. This is simply the biological economics of physics. Bird droppings on new cars are trickle-down economics. If you lose sleep over bird droppings, acid rain will kill you for sure. The EPA explains it this way: High emission = acid rain x poor paint jobs ÷ accelerated depreciation + or - road salt/bird droppings = automaker profits + additional high emissions.

• English sparrows and starlings have been wildly successful since their introduction to North America and have become a destructive nuisance to native wildlife.

• Birdfeeders made of metal, plastic, or glass, with nonporous surfaces, are easiest to keep clean.

• You can sometimes scare unwanted birds off with a plastic owl. There is no fool like an owl fool.

• Salmonellosis (sal-muh-nel-LOW-sis) is a general term for any disease caused by a group of bacteria known by the Latin name Salmonella. It can quickly kill birds. Abscesses often form in the lining of the esophagus as part of the infection process. Infected birds pass bacteria in their fecal droppings. Other birds get sick when they eat food contaminated by the droppings. Salmonellosis is the most common birdfeeding disease. There is only one way to prevent salmonellosis: Clean your feeders often!

Dear Dick E. Bird

Dear Dick E. Bird:

How do I break my cat from getting into my birdfeeder?
— Feline Feuding in Philly

Dear Philly:

Breaking your cat of eating your birds and breaking your heart is impossible unless you confine the cat.

Birds and cats do not mix. It is very natural for cats to stalk birds. It is not their fault if they get your birds; it is your fault.

A bell is not the answer and don't let anyone tell you it is — unless you use the Liberty Bell. The bell is often the last sound a songbird will hear. If you decide to try a bell, use at least two bells on the cat's collar. But the only foolproof solution is to keep your cats indoors and your birds outdoors.

Many people will swear that their cats do not stalk birds — this is wishful thinking and major shrinking from the responsibility to protect songbirds. Cats make excellent bird-watchers, but you have to make sure it is through a window. This, of course, will make your male cats Peeping Toms, but it will spare some of the millions of songbirds taken annually by wild and pet domestic cats.

— Keep Smilin', Dick E. Bird

Dear Dick E. Bird:

I can find a million books on how to attract birds, feed them, house them, and landscape for them. Why can't I find one on how to get along with them, now that I have them. They get up early and make all kinds of racket. They act like no one else has a right to sleep. I need help. —Early Bird in Battle Creek

Dear Bird Battle:

It sounds like you might be out of luck (with birds you have to take the good with the bad) , but let me suggest you use a little psychology before you try a psychiatrist. Fight fire with fire. Set your alarm and get up earlier than your birds. Go outside and sing to them. This approach could backfire if your neighbors are close by and you may be experiencing post-molt syndrome. Birds are very quiet when they molt. Once the molted plumage is replaced, they make up for lost time. You might think it's spring all over again. Be patient and try to enjoy the beautiful sounds your birds are capable of making. There is truly no sound more refreshing in the entire world.

— Keep Smilin', Dick E. Bird

Dear Dick E. Bird:

I used to think I only had to worry about critters stealing my birdseed after I put it outside. My bushy-tails have become much bolder. I recently went out and found my fifty-pound bags of sunflower hearts broken into. Actually, they were chewed into. There was seed scattered all over my garage. Any suggestions on storing seed so I won't have to hire a Pinkerton person?

— Broken-Hearted in Harrisburg

Dear Broken:

I hope you haven't already gone out and bought a plastic garbage can. This is the mistake many people make before realizing that raiding rodents chew through a plastic garbage can and think of it as an appetizer. I strongly recommend storing seed in a safety deposit box, but if that is not convenient, a large-capacity metal garbage can with an extra-tight lid is the next best option. You can recover most of the stolen loot if the mice have taken it. You will find it under the hood of your car, in stored ski boots, your fuse box, and under your dog's dish.

— Keep Smilin', Dick E. Bird

Tongue-in-Beak Tidbits

Experience is the best teacher, and you will not have to feed birds very long to experience all the problems discussed in this chapter. Keep your head down and your chin up, your nose clean and your ears open. When the going gets tough, the tough get going — so get going!

APPLY FEATHERED FACTS

1. What makes up a good percentage of a hawk's diet?
2. What is another name for a woodpecker's "drumming" on objects?
3. Why are hawks considered greedy?
4. How do you describe the story of a hawk taking songbirds from feed stations?

DISCUSSION TOPICS

1. What do you call a squirrel's eating procedure?
2. What is an eavesdropper?
3. What do you call the horrible scene when a cat attacks songbirds?
4. If there are eight birds on your feeder and a cat gets one, how many remain?

BIRD-BRAINED TRIVIA

1. What movie had the largest dry-cleaning bill in the history of filmmaking?
2. Should you use a wedge to get a squirrel out of a squirrel-proof birdfeeder?
3. What bird is also known as the "sparrow hawk"?
4. Does a shrike use its strong talons to snatch other songbirds at the birdfeeder?
5. What is the best cover you can offer songbirds within close proximity to the feeder?
6. What is the most miserable cat to deal with that shows up at feed stations?
7. What is the best way to keep seed from sprouting under seed dispensers?

AND THE ANSWER IS—

Apply Feathered Facts: 1. Songbirds and rodents. 2. Tattooing. 3. Because if you give them a finch, they will take the whole yard. 4. Gripping. **Discussion Topics:** 1. Inhaling. 2. A bird that sits on your rain gutter and poops on your house. 3. Cat-e-gory. 4. None. The other seven left, and they won't be back. **Bird-Brained Trivia:** 1. The Birds. 2. No, a nine iron is much more effective. 3. American kestrel. 4. No, a shrike does not have talons. But it does have strong feet and sharp claws that work just as well. 5. Thick conifers and dense shrubs. 6. Polecat. 7. Catch trays and regular cleaning.

She left the future stranded there,
'Twas a fairly small depression.
With never a guilt, a backward glance,
And never a thought of confession.
To give away the rights of birth,
Seems naturally absurd.
But life begins in a stranger's nest,
For every new cowbird.

—DICK E. BIRD

Bird Droppings

The following are all observations you can experience in your own backyard if you stop, look, and listen!

• A bird's claws, like human fingernails, grow continuously. In the wild they do not have a chance to grow long because the birds are always working their fingers to the bone, trying to make ends meet and keeping their mouths full. This helps keep their stomachs full, which keeps their claws growing. It's just one vicious circle.

• With no tools but beaks, birds construct nests that endure rain, wind, and all other elements. These nests conserve heat and hold restless young'uns.

87

• When a bird stands on a perch, its weight tightens the tendons so that the feet lock around the perch. This enables the bird to sleep on its feet.

• In preparation for their migration flight, some songbirds will eat until they double their weight.

• All birds suffer from ailurophobia. (Fear of cats.)

• Grosbeaks have bills that are particularly well adapted to feeding on seeds and are even strong enough to crack cherry pits to get the nourishment inside.

• The brown creeper, unlike a nuthatch, only moves up a tree, looking for a meal. Once it reaches the top, it does not call the fire department but instead flies to the bottom of another tree and starts up again. Ornithologically, this is known as "starting at the bottom and working your way up."

• You can entice cedar waxwings to your feeder with raisins and chopped apples.

• Birds like to preen where they have a good unobstructed view in all directions. There is nothing worse than being attacked when you have your head under your armpit, or someplace else inconvenient.

• Birds have two eyelids: upper and lower. This enables them to wink north and south.

• A bird's daily food intake is tied closely to the temperature. In cold weather birds eat more. Other factors are health, age, sex, season, and availability. Many birds will be attracted to your feeder only when you're running specials on suet or some premium mix, while others could care less and will eat anything that does not eat them first.

• Aspergillosis, caused by a fungus or mold, is a sickness your birds can contract from a dirty feeder or birdbath. It is very important to clean your feeders and baths regularly. Birds breathe in the spores of this mold, which can lead to avian pneumonia.

• Your birdbath should be shallow enough so that your birds can use it without a snorkel. I recommend approximately two inches of water so they can splash around.

• The sound of running or splashing water will attract many birds.

• One way to get brown creepers to come to your birdfeeder is by adding chopped peanuts, suet mix, peanut butter and cornmeal, to your menu.

• Digestion in songbirds is very rapid. Once they partake of your sunflower seed—it's history. In less than two hours that seed is fertilizer. If you watch your birds carefully, you will notice they are very efficient. They are flying production lines. They are constantly taking in seed at one end and producing fertilizer at the other. But if you are observant, you will also notice that a small amount of waste is generated from a large amount of food intake. Most of what a bird eats is turned into the energy it requires to survive and maintain its high body temperature.

• Birds such as the robin, tree swallow, and phoebe have been known to build their nests and raise their young on moving ferryboats.

• Male and female robins have been known to feed the young of other birds.

• A ruby-throated hummingbird, weighing in at less than one ounce, can fly nonstop across the Gulf of Mexico.

• The male winter wren builds the nest by himself and then puts on his displays to attract a female to it. Once the female is incubating, he may go on to build another nest and find another mate. This is called "two-timing" in ornithological lingo. It's no wonder he spends so much time creeping through the low, dense tangle of brush and branches.

• Camouflage is a very important part of nest building. Using material that blends with the surroundings is quite normal. Some birds build near stinging insect nests for added security.

• Barn swallows make over one thousand flights, each time carrying a tiny pellet of mud, to build a single nest.

• The average robin requires seventy worms a day, which is the reason they rise so early.

• A bird can focus its eye more quickly than any other living creature.

• The kiss is not the sole property of the human species. Birds use their bills as a form of caress.

• Before a baby bird is hatched, it has a temporary tooth that enables it to break out of the egg.

• Owls can swivel their heads 270 degrees of the full 360 degrees. They swivel their heads so fast that some people think they can spin them all the way around.

• An oriole takes as many as twelve days to weave its hanging nest.

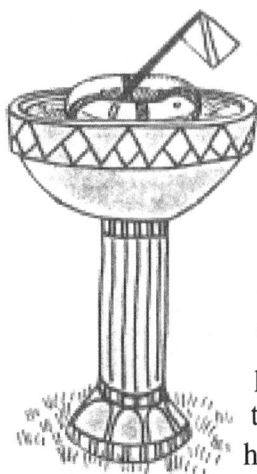

• The great horned owl is said to be one of the few animals that will eat a skunk. They will eat the whole thing—hook, line, and stinker.

• A mockingbird has been known to change its tune eighty-seven times in seven minutes. For sheer variety, inventiveness, composition, and creation, no bird can equal the mocker. At 5:30 A.M., however, they have many critics.

• Doves are one of the few species of birds that suck up water like a horse, instead of taking a billful and letting it trickle down the throat.

• The fastest-running flying bird is the roadrunner. It has been clocked racing a car at 28 miles per hour. Its extended wings act as stabilizers.

• A baby bird takes its first breath from the air stored in the blunt end of the egg.

• The sapsucker has a method all its own for collecting sap. It taps trees by drilling holes in orderly rows that circle the trunk. It comes back often to drink at its wells and keep the sap flowing.

• Nighthawks eat hundreds of insects per hour. They are sometimes called "mosquito hawks" or "bull bats."

• An adult barn owl will eat approximately twenty-three to twenty-five mice per night, give or take a mouse.

• The great crested flycatcher and the tufted titmouse often use snakeskin in their nests. Possibly for the mere purpose of adornment.

• The crossbill is one bird that can survive very well in a coniferous forest. Its crossed and pointed beak design helps it get at the seeds that are inside cones.

• Hummingbird wings are almost rigid and swivel at the shoulders.

• The roadrunner has the speed and agility to capture most fast-moving lizards and snakes.

• Woodpeckers are one of the few birds that will maintain a dwelling all year long.

• The cedar waxwing came by its name because the tips of some of the wing feathers resemble sealing wax. It is one of the finest tailored birds in the skies.

• California has more varieties of woodpeckers than any other state.

• Without exception, birds come from eggs, but where do eggs come from?

• The bobolink gets so fat before it flies south for the winter. It is sometimes called the "butterbird."

• The hummingbird is a feathered prism—a living rainbow. Hummers get their metallic look from tiny barbs on each little plumule of every feather that is channeled to break and refract the light, just as a cut diamond does.

• Given by both sexes, bird calls are short, nonmusical vocalizations that function to communicate information about daily activities, such as feeding, flocking, migration, and alarm. When you first put out a birdfeeder, you will hear a universal call "Come and get it!" This is the only call common to all backyard birds.

• A woodpecker can build a nesting site in a healthy hardwood tree. This job requires a beak equipped with an extremely hard sheath and a special edge with a chisel-shaped point.
• Male songbirds will use their splendid colors, peculiar dance steps, and beautiful song to entice the females. It is usually a short

engagement. There is too much work to be done for long-drawn-out relationships.

• Hummingbirds, in courtship flight, will do loop-de-loops, sharp curves, and repeatedly stop in midair and face each other.

• Hummingbirds can achieve practically full speed at the instant they take off.

• Flickers love ants. Ants make up a large portion of their diet.

• The feathers of most birds weigh more than their skeletons. In the case of birds of prey, the feathers will weigh almost twice as much.

• A bird's pectoral muscles make up over 20 percent of its overall body weight.

• Birds use their tail feathers for steering, braking, and stabilization.

• If you ever wondered how birds wash those hard-to-reach spots—they preen each other, as well as themselves. Dirty feathers can cause flight problems and loss of body heat.

• In two or three weeks, naked little songbird babies will sprout several thousand feathers. It's hard to believe this beautiful plumage comes from stuffing worms, bugs, and veggies into those gaping little bills.

• The meadowlark builds its nest on the ground in true Frank Lloyd Wright tradition. It arches grasses over the nest to hide and weatherproof.

• It is believed that chickadees can live up to ten years in the wild; twenty if they can get on Medicare.

• A woodpecker has a mean tongue from an insect's point of view. It has a long reach and is equipped with a spiny tip, like a harpoon.

• Two-thirds of the young birds that reach flying age die in the first year.

"Let's just go to Brazil and stay there this time."

• Birds do not have reverse. They do not seem to be able to walk backward.

• Some birds like the city life and find that every automobile is a potential meal. They have learned to climb into the grill area and pick insects off the radiator. It is very convenient and the insects are always grilled to perfection.

• Cedar waxwings can store an enormous amount of fruit in their crops and regurgitate the contents all at once to their young.

• Birds start breathing a day or so before hatching. (They probably just want to try some good air before they come out of their shells.)

• American goldfinches weave a nest of plant fibers and thistledown so tightly that it will hold water.

• The chipping sparrow is also nicknamed the "hairbird" because of its habit of lining nests with horsehair—or any other hair it can find.

• It takes the American redstart male a year before he develops his beautiful coat of bright orange.

• A bird's head is made up of five bones: one frontal, two sideals, one topal, and a backal.

• Swallows change direction almost constantly.

They buzz and flap, flitter and flit,
Eat all day and seldom sit.
And when they do, they don't sit still,
It seems a regimented drill.
And now they have me moving too,
Providing all their treats.
But now my life is such a joy,
Observing all their feats— Wings too!
—Dick E. Bird

• When a bird is flying forward, only the downstroke of the wings gives it propulsion. Both the upstroke and downstroke give the bird lift.

• A natural winter food source for chickadees is insect eggs, or larvae of insects, hidden in bark crevices.

• A jay's diet during spring and summer consists of approximately 40 percent animal foods. Much of this ends up being baby birds robbed from nests.

• The Anna's hummingbird is the most common garden hummer in California. It eats more tiny insects than any other hummer.

• Many birds, including jays and owls, will eat frogs if the opportunity presents itself. This is why you hear frogs croaking at night so much. It's their way of having roll call to see who has croaked and who's still croaking.

• Birds have a very unique breathing system. They breathe in and out, just like we do, but the air does not go only into their lungs. It also goes into their hollow bones. A bird's heart pumps blood quickly around the body. All of these functions help keep a bird warm. This is the reason you will seldom see a bird with battery-operated socks. Feathers also help insulate.

• There are over 1,800 species of fleas in the world. Of these, only about 100 species have been reported on birds.

• Common redpolls are very tame birds and often caught by hand at window feeders by bird-banders.

• A full-grown human would have to eat forty pounds of food a day to match what a songbird needs during a typical winter day.

• House finches were once found only in the West. They were sold as pets in the East as "Hollywood finches" and released when the Migratory Bird Act was passed.

• A woodpecker's tongue is so long that it must curl around the inside of its head. When a woodpecker has something on his mind it's usually his tongue.

• Most desert birds get the water they need from the food they eat, rather than by drinking. (They always look for a mouse with a canteen.)

• A cactus wren, which is about the size of a sparrow, builds a nest about the size of a football.

• Bird-banders use fine silk-mesh nets called mist nets. Birds become entangled in these nets but are easily removed without injury.

• Some birds will sunbathe to get rid of parasites. The sun raises their body temperature and drives the parasites to within striking distance.

• Both the male and female cardinal sing — often together. They make a nice couple and are probably one of the most admired North American songbirds.

• Shrikes feed on insects, rodents, and small birds. They quite often hang their prey on thorns until they are ready to dine.

• The cooing made by mourning doves comes from the male and female.

• Most birds have extremely keen vision. One pair of eyes may combine both telescopic and microscopic ability. One reason for such good vision is the relatively large size of a bird's eyes. Each eye is often as large as the bird's brain. If our eyes were the size of our brain, we would probably be blind.

• Feathers keep birds warm even in the harshest conditions. Birds fluff their feathers when it's cold, creating pockets of warm air trapped in the feathers. The "down" feathers close to the body are very efficient at trapping air.

• Roadrunners, members of the cuckoo family, are seldom found in clocks because they always run fast.

• The raven is the largest member of the crow family. Its specific name is corax, which is Greek for croaker.

• Birds are the most useful animals for man. We eat them before they are born and after they are dead.

• Starlings and English sparrows will steal worms directly from a robin's beak.

• The cardinal has at least two dozen variations of its whistle song.

• The phoebe will sometimes say his name thirty or forty times a minute— or until he gets it right.

• According to some experts, the average number of eggs laid by songbirds tends to be larger in northern latitudes.

• Hummingbirds have the greatest energy output—by weight—of any other warm-blooded creature.

• Snakes will climb trees and bushes to get bird eggs and young.

• All perching birds have altricial young that are helpless at birth and remain in the nest until they are able to straighten up and fly right.

• Many birds carry the groceries home in their stomachs. This way they can regurgitate it for their young. This may sound a little gross, but actually it helps the young by having food already partially digested.

• A roadrunner can dodge a rattlesnake's lightning bite and at the right moment hammer its bill into the snake's skull. The bird then swallows the snake whole. (This explains why they are part of the cuckoo family.)

• A hummingbird has short legs and eight toes (four on each foot); you can see them by holding your eyeballs still when observing this bird.

• A bird can move each feather independently by contracting specific muscles near the base of the feather.

• Seagulls fluttering behind a farmer's plow have often been called "prairie doves."

• Killdeer are very independent and will usually not make use of any food supplies you provide them. They nest where they want, when they want, and expect you to drive, walk, and mow around them. Killdeer are selective insect eaters. They will dine on mosquitoes, beetles, ticks, and flies.

• Woodpeckers do not kill the trees they feed upon.

• Mourning doves feed their young something called "crop milk," a yogurt-like substance.

• There are more cervical vertebra in the neck of a bird than the neck of a giraffe. A sparrow has fourteen, a swan has twenty-three. A giraffe, who is always bragging about his neck, only has seven.

• Turkey vultures are very valuable birds. They dine on and quickly dispose of carcasses that would otherwise spread disease.

• Many birds begin life in a depression (in the ground). Ground-nesting birds are usually a blend of soft colors so that they are concealed from predators.

• Earthworms have a lot of nutritional value. I don't mean to tempt you, and the birds certainly do not need the competition, but worms are very high in protein when fresh.

• Birds have eyelashes, in a sense. They are modified featherlike bristles.

• The predominant aerodynamic forces — lift and drag — that act on an airplane in flight work the same way on a bird. It grabs hold of all the seed it can. If the bird can lift it, it can drag it home.

• All birds, except the hummingbird, can move their wings from the shoulders, elbows, and wrists. Yes, birds have all these parts; they just look different.

• Kingbirds are very aggressive. They have been known to attack hawks, vultures, and even airplanes that enter their nesting airspace without proper clearance.

• Walk, run, and hop — most birds use one or more of these transportation methods when not in flight.

• Birds are imprinted at birth. They have their little brains stamped with special instructions on how to act. After that they can be as creative as they wish.

• On cold but sunny winter days, a road-runner is thought to use solar energy to warm up and reduce its food requirements. What it does is erect its back feathers to expose normally covered areas of black skin to the sun. (This is ornithologically called "mooning the sun.") The black skin rapidly absorbs the warmth of the sun and, when sufficiently "solar charged," the bird depresses the feathers covering the skin and goes about discharging his duties.

• Migration is the label attached to birds that move annually and seasonally, although many birds migrate sporadically, partially, locally, and irruptively.

• Since the forelimbs of birds are adapted for flying, it is necessary for them to have well-developed bills and feet for grasping and holding food — and also as their chief weapons for defense.

• Little birds have big eggs, and big birds have little eggs, in proportion to their body weights.

• "Birds of a feather flock together." This is true, but winter flocks often consist of mixed company. A variety of birds will hang in winter flocks and congregate at concentrations of food, like your feeder.

• The crop of a bird can act as a food-storage area, sound device, and a darned good place to keep valuables.

• Birds do not need deodorant because they do not have sweat glands. They are panters and lose a lot of their body heat by using their respiratory systems.

• Newly hatched birds develop quickly. They will often double their weight in one day.

• At least 200 species of birds are known to eat dragonflies, which makes dragonflies very nervous.

• The size of a ruby-throated hummingbird's nest is about as big as a thimble. It is made of lichen and other small pieces of plant material. It looks like a bump on a log and is very hard to locate—unless you're a hummingbird.

• The dictionary defines a bird's "habitat" as "all the elements and conditions that satisfy the living requirements of a bird, so that it can successfully produce offspring in sufficient numbers to perpetuate its kind."

• The name grosbeak comes from the words "gross" and "beak." There was that chance that we could have had stoutbeaks or massivebeaks feeding outside our kitchen windows instead. However, through the process of vocabulary roulette, we have grosbeaks.

• It is very important for birds to guard their nests even before eggs are placed in them. There is no honor among thieves, and many birds would rather use materials already collected than to go searching for their own.

• Nuthatches work a tree differently from other birds. They search tree bark from the top down, giving them a different angle on bugs hiding in the bark that other birds miss.

• The cardinal's bill works a lot like a nutcracker. It has a grooved upper bill and a sharp lower bill. Watch the lower bill, or mandible, when it is eating seed. The lower half moves forward and breaks open the seed.

"If I could get a little more time off, I'd go with them this winter."

The cardinal can then shuck off the hard cover and eat the meat. Birds have very talented mouths.

• The white-crowned sparrow spends a lot of time in the lab. Much of what we know about the physiology of bird migration comes from experimenting with this species.

• The cowbird is also known as the "buffalo bird." These birds used to follow the massive herds of buffalo and feed off the insects they stirred up.

• Hummingbirds can come to a full stop without any braking distance. If a plane tried to stop as fast, it would lose its wings, engine, passengers, and luggage. Actually, a plane can lose luggage without stopping.

• Even though the mourning dove is most active in the morning, its name comes from its sad call, not its early hours.

• The belted kingfisher is found all over North America. Its nest is burrowed into a bank near water. It has tunnel vision.

• The purple martin is the largest swallow in North America.

• The American crow is totally black—feet, body, and bill.

• The male house wren will build several dummy nests. Some say these are used for decoys, while others contend he is trying to give the female a choice— — and she thinks *he's* a dummy . . .

• The gray catbird often mimics other birds, and even an occasional tree frog. So if you hear a tree frog croak, it could be a catbird. If you hear an alarm clock, train whistle, or catbird, it could be a mockingbird. Many tree frogs stutter because every time they try to express themselves, they are cut off by some pushy bird with a speech disorder.

• A good whippoorwill is heard but not often seen. It is rarely seen because it sleeps all day, well camouflaged on the forest floor, and works the night shift, catching insects and making sure the whole world knows how to pronounce its name.

• Flocks of goldfinches are appropriately called "charms."

• Young birds often produce their droppings in a kind of natural sandwich bag. This clear sac makes the droppings manageable for adults to then remove the droppings from the nest area, or eat them so that predators are not attracted to the young by accumulated waste.

• Young waxwings are raised almost exclusively on insects, but once on their own, their diet gradually changes to fruit.

And So It Goes

First, a little algae in a pond goes floating by,
And asks a little water flea what it's like to fly.
The water flea knew little and never had he flew,
But he ate the little algae, that is how he grew.

A minnow happened through the weeds,
And spied the flea that grew.
He sucked him in a great big gulp,
He didn't even chew.

Before the flea could settle in
With others who'd been ate,
Along came fish of greater size,
Who sealed the minnow's fate.

It was a happy, healthy fish,
Who ate the minnow whole.
He thought he ruled the universe,
Till nature took its toll.

Basking in the sun alone
Digesting his last meal,
An osprey glided overhead,
And gave that fish a feel.

It was a strange sensation,
As they raced into the sky.
But now that little algae knows,
What it's like to fly.

— Dick E. Bird

• A bird's brain is so complicated and complex that it has been described as a switchboard. Information is sorted and sent to the right department. The problem is that many times there is a busy signal, and by the time the information makes it to the brain the bird has already done something stupid like flying into a picture window.

• In the past, red-shouldered and red-tailed hawks were often mislabeled "hen hawks," shot down, and nailed to barn doors. It took education to convince farmers that these birds consumed mainly rodents and that they were good for their farms.

• State birds are chosen by state legislatures, state commissions, governors' proclamations, unofficially, popular vote, schoolchildren, and garden clubs.

• At least forty-five species of North American birds eat lizards. Twenty-six species of North American birds eat snakes. This is proof that more birds prefer their reptiles with legs than without.

• Hummingbirds will sometimes become trapped in spider webs.

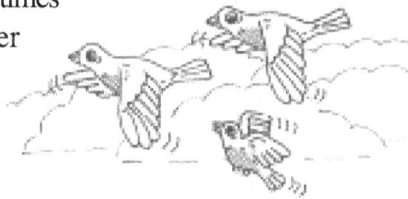

• European settlers were at first very beneficial to the Eastern bluebird. The forests they cleared opened much preferred habitat for these birds. At the same time the settlers introduced starlings

"Next can we try a little parallel parking, Dad?"

107

and house sparrows, which proved to be overwhelming competition for nesting habitat.

• One learning behavior of birds is trial and error. Learning to fly comes naturally, but proficiency is no different from your kid learning to drive a car.

• Native Americans used to hang out hollowed gourds to attract martins. These birds consume huge numbers of flying insects.

• It is believed that cliff swallows share information on food location.

• Cracked corn is one of the biggest wild bird food sellers because of its low cost, and it also is high in nutritional value.

• Common redpolls come from their breeding grounds in the Canadian tundra and are often regular visitors at feed stations in southern Canada and the Northern tier states in the United States. You will find them hanging out in large groups of mixed finches and chickadees.

• Birds use many methods to protect their eggs and young. Many use camouflage. Others burrow in the ground and hide their eggs there. Some like to nest high in trees with a bird's-eye view. Many birds nest in tangled thickets that make predator approach difficult.

• Baby crows will not foul their nest. As soon as they are able to move about, but still unable to fly, baby crows will move to the edge of the nest, turn tail downwind, and let 'er fly. Now, is that smart or what?

Imagination was given to man to compensate him for what he is not; a sense of humor to console him for what his squirrels do to his birdfeeder.

—Dick E. Bird

4 •

Squirrelly Neighbors

Don't Make a Big Hairy Deal
Out of Your Squirrels

I have been covering the squirrel beat for years, and I have heard most of the usual methods of foiling squirrels.

People love to hate their squirrels and hate to love their squirrels, but the best thing you can do is to get used to them. One thing you should know right up front before you get too deep into feeding birds— half of everything you spend goes directly into a squirrel's savings account. You can believe all those fairy tales about squirrel-proof feeders if it makes you feel better, but reality will set in every day you go out and find a furball sitting inside one of them.

Don't Make Your Squirrel Into A Big Hairy Deal

A squirrel is a born swindler who can con a corn kernel from a canary. A herd of squirrels is sometimes known as a "dray." This is rather amusing because a dray is defined as "a low cart without fixed sides, for carrying heavy loads." How appropriate. Bank robber Willie Sutton was once asked why he robbed banks. "Because that's where the money is," he said. Same goes for your squirrel. Opportunity makes the thief and that's it in a nutshell.

Nothing in Life Is Guaranteed Except Squirrels Eating Birdseed

Squirrels are very talented members of the animal kingdom. If you've ever watched them, you've noticed they always try to keep something between them and you — and usually it's your birdfeeder. Through the process of evolution, they have developed one of the most amazing eating stances in the world of nature.

Squirrels sit at birdfeeders with their feet dug into the launch position and their bodies facing down range. They chew birdseed at a speed that

> *Possession is nine-tenths of the law at the birdfeeder.*

cannot be accurately recorded and at the same time are able to keep one eye totally dedicated to watching the windows of the house.

It doesn't bother a squirrel one bit as long as he can see you, but once you go out of sight this little furball shifts into second gear. This is the anticipation stance.

The leg muscles tense and adrenaline pumps through the whole body. When it hits the brain, the ears stiffen straight up. By the time you hit the front steps at a full gallop, that squirrel power-shifts into third.

His tail curls into a tuck, blood's pumping to peak launch-pressure levels, and nerve endings quiver from battling with the brain over the decision to stay and eat one more seed or launch now, lunch later. When you finally break around the corner of the house, the brain gives in to the nerves, and the squirrel jumps all the way to the neighbor's feeder.

It is totally amazing. Do not let these squirrels cause you mental stress. You may want to start a support group with other neighbors so you can let your frustrations out and discuss freely the feelings you are experiencing.

There are hundreds of squirrel-preventative formulas and contraptions, most of which I've found are incredibly useless. Some squirrels are so defiant that they eat in a combat-readiness stance.

You can forget window knocking and broom chasing as possible solutions. You will only end up with sore knuckles and cramps. There are two types of equipment used to combat squirrels — manned and unmanned. The drawback with manned squirrel equipment is that it is very labor-intensive. For instance, you can drive your squirrels away with a remote-controlled, battery-operated dune buggy. You control it from the kitchen. Just back it into the bushes and when a squirrel heads for the birdfeeder, you peel out. Chase him all the way to the neighbor's yard, then back it into the bushes and wait.

Another option is a baby monitor. The nice thing about a baby monitor is that a squirrel can't talk back to you. It is a one-way listening device. You put the sound unit on the birdfeeder and watch from the house. When that little furball climbs up and starts eating — be patient. Let him relax a bit. When he first perches himself up on the feeder, he is real nervous. His jaws move very rapidly and so do his eyes. You should be able to see when he starts to relax. His chewing slows and his tail lowers to half-mast. That's when you turn on the monitor and yell at him. He should go off like the Challenger spacecraft and hit the ground running. It's not very nice, but you will have this warm glow about you.

Squirrelly Apparatus

Weight-activated squirrel-proof birdfeeder contraptions work and will keep mentally challenged squirrels out of your seed. Since half the squirrel population suffers from various forms of learning disabilities, that means a 50 percent seed savings. But there is a fine line between a genius and an idiot. Squirrels live on that line. This is the reason your squirrels possess a dichotomy of abilities. Before buying a squirrel baffle or squirrel-proof feeder, it is always wise to check the skill level of your squirrels to see if the darn thing will even work.

> *A squirrel by any other name is still a seed-stealing thief.*

The original weight-activated squirrel-proof feeder had an adjustable weight connected to the perch shelf. This device, like the spring-activated types, will discourage a fat squirrel or nine average-size chickadees. My squirrels take turns. One sits on the back, holding it open while the other one eats, then they switch.

When placing these unique devices, you must also be careful not to put it close enough to a tree or hedge a squirrel can jump from. I had a squirrel who would jump inside the feeder, never even touching the weight-activated perch. Once inside, he was high and dry sitting on a week's supply of groceries. It wasn't until he came out that he hit the perch and it closed on his tail. He thought someone had grabbed him by the heinie. Going absolutely bonkers, he ended up back inside the feeder looking out to see who it was that had him. He did this three times until he finally fell out instead of back in. One woman saw a squirrel dive in her birdfeeder, so she took her husband's nine iron and "rang his bell." Probably ruined her husband's golf club and a $70 birdfeeder too.

Stupid squirrels will sit on the closed perch for hours scratching their heads. The smart ones will rip you off and leave you scratching your head.

Squirrel Sight Chart

Scientists are still trying to determine if squirrels can actually read and pretend to be illiterate, or if they are actually illiterate and pretend to read. From various studies designed to determine the reading skills of squirrels, it appears the rodents can read minds—both shallow and deep—but there is no evidence they can actually read sentences. Tests show a certain amount of recognition of several common words, like "sunflower," "seed," and "corn." Using a peanut bag as an eye chart, most squirrels are able to read even the fine print at the bottom of the bag.

"Chill out, Ernie, it's just a game."

115

Squirrellyosis

One of the most important things to remember about squirrels is their ability to make a perfectly normal, even-tempered human being go nutso. You can let them eat all your birdseed, you can watch them destroy a new $50 feeder, but never let them drive you over the hedge.

It is now a known fact that a newly discovered, stress-related disease called "squirrellyosis" is showing up in many parts of the country. If not treated it causes a deranged condition, beginning with screaming and yelling while pounding on the windows. If you see this behavior in a loved one, it would be best to seek professional help immediately.

If anyone you know begins to show symptoms of squirrellyosis, it might be best to try to reason with him early about seeking help. Once he is to the point of bolting through the door and chasing furballs through the yard, making karate-like noises, it is most likely that permanent damage has been done.

There is therapy now being tested that could help even the most severe cases of squirrellyosis. It is still in the experimental stages but involves placing patients in a backyard setting, with a squirrel at a feeding station, and counseling them on mind-control methods. As they progress, the sessions are extended. In some cases people who have been afflicted can watch a squirrel eat birdseed for twenty to thirty minutes without showing any signs of homicidal tendencies.

With the right grass-roots programs, this disease could be nipped in the bud. Don't think that this could not happen to you. The disease strikes without warning and can have a lasting effect on you and your family.

Scientists advocate passing out surplus government grain to those people with the worst cases. This, they feel, would help relieve their emotional stress until further studies can be made and programs implemented. At this time those people needing and seeking help have to wait six months to get into a program. By that time they are so squirrelly, it is just too darn late to help them.

Researchers continue to search for a breakthrough in this fight to save seed and sanity all over the world.

Tactical Maneuvers

If your squirrels are overrunning your perimeter, stop feeding for a while. Your attempt to keep up the supply of seed is only fueling their population. Let them work for a living for a little while. Only the strong will survive. The others will go someplace else. You are always going to have squirrels. They are a big part of enjoying birdfeeding. When they begin to take over everything you put out for the birds, it doesn't take long to tire of them. Nothing is worse than putting out a nice new feeder and having some little furball eat a hole in it on the first day. Just as OPEC affects gas prices, which in turn affects motorists, you will find squirrels become less organized as the supply dwindles. They begin squabbling among themselves and fighting while in line. This is very basic squirrel psychology, so it's important that you control the seed supply. Live-trapping is also an alternative, but make sure you release them away from any main roads and blindfold them during transport. Many times they will hitchhike back before lunch.

It's so relaxing here by the feeder."

117

Croplifting

Squirrels have sticky fingers and are known to be the most compulsive "croplifters." Crime pays a handsome dividend to a rodent with a will and a ground squirrel with a goal. As more and more people throw up their hands and learn to enjoy their squirrels, squirrels have switched tactics from "hit-and-run" to "sit-and-sun."

One out of every three people feeding birds now owns at least one squirrel feeder. Squirrel toy sales are also on the rise. Teeter-totters, swings, whirl-your-rodents, and peanut boxes are selling like seedcakes.

Rodent

The word "rodent" comes from a Latin word meaning "to gnaw," and gnawing is what squirrels do best. Unless your squirrels have been to the orthodontist, you will notice that their four front teeth are designed especially for gnawing. Their teeth grow like fingernails. Squirrels will chew up a feeder just to get the last, hard-to-reach seed in the very bottom. The solution to this problem is easy. Keep the feeder full. Many studies have shown that a squirrel not able to get at the last bit of seed will either chew a hole or use plastic explosives.

You will find squirrels at your feeders throughout the year. They do not hibernate. They remain active except during extremely cold weather, when they hole up to conserve energy.

The biggest problem with squirrels is that they do not come with instructions. They can be very confusing even to themselves. Squirrels are tone-deaf and cannot hear the sound made by pounding on window glass. It is hard to tell a male from a female — and even an innie from an outie. Some squirrels will sit on the outside of a birdfeeder and reach in, preferring to eat out, while others like to climb into a birdfeeder to eat in when they are eating out.

The reason so many squirrels are killed by automobiles is indecisiveness. A squirrel has a very dominant tail. It actually pushes the squirrel's body wherever it wants to go. If a squirrel is in the middle of the road when a car is coming, the tail usually wants to go one way and the body another. By the time they get their differences worked out it's often too late.

Honor Among Thieves

You can't say squirrels are lazy, stupid, or unimaginative. Every rascal is not a thief, but every thief is a rascal. The tricky part is figuring out if your squirrels are thieves or rascals. There is always honor among thieves. So if your squirrel looks honorable, you still might have a problem. The birdfeeder would be a dull place without a few squirrel brawls once in a while to keep things lively. This is not to say you should let down your guard. It is your duty to try keeping furballs off your feeder. If you didn't try, they would be disappointed, and there would probably be rioting. They don't always like the competition, but they look forward to the challenge.

Squirrels trying to eke a living out of your backyard really have it tough. They come from a long line of zigzaggers, and the nut never falls far from the family tree. Besides the broom-wielding madwoman who hides around the corner of the house, a squirrel has to worry about being ambushed by bobcats, coyotes, foxes, hawks, and domestic pets.

Do you ever wonder why they peek around a tree at you and scream obscenities? It's because they have been shot at ever since

119

they made our acquaintance. Squirrels at one time were such a problem to pioneer farmers' crops that colonial governments accepted squirrel scalps for payment of taxes. We can thank squirrels for turning colonists from crackpots into crack shots, devastating the British ranks during the American Revolution.

Nutcracker Suite

Tree cavities are a squirrel's number-one choice for affordable housing, but in this day and age a good hole is hard to find. Developers and woodcutters have eliminated much of these choice spots. Most of the squirrels that cannot find decent attics to live in will weave nests of leaves that are easy to spot in the winter silhouettes of trees.

These bulky bungalows are waterproof and roomy enough for company. That's right, squirrels need lovin' too. They have two litters of critters a year.

Squirrel Vision

Trying to watch squirrels without their knowing it has permanently affected many people who feed birds. The eyes are the first to go, and most experts agree that the constant strain on the directional eye muscles causes them to fatigue and involuntarily relax in a left or right position. Most agree that if patients would face their squirrels and stare directly at them, this condition would never develop. You can tell when a person first begins to show signs of squirrel vision. It usually happens when he or she is paying for seed at the cash register. Suddenly they will stand sideways and talk out of the side of their mouth. Don't embarrass this person by asking if he has squirrel vision, because he could just be stunned from seeing the seed bill. Studies are beginning to show that this is not just a physical problem; it's also psychological. Even with optic exercise, the treatment to correct this condition is not always totally successful. Many people just cannot bring themselves to face their squirrels, and the side-eye condition becomes dominant again as soon as they get back home. Doctors are recommending that patients move to a part of the country where squirrels are less abundant.

Surefooted

Have you ever seen squirrels fall? They fall often, but that does not mean they are not surefooted; it means they push themselves to do the impossible. A squirrel is one of the most confident critters in the animal kingdom. Wire walking and branch hopping are as natural as eating or sleeping to a squirrel. Squirrels can take falls of hundreds of feet and land as easily as a bird. That might be stretching it a bit, but after a thud, they always run. On the way down, they have this panicked look on their faces, and I am sure they are screaming on the inside. But squirrels are proud and wouldn't want anyone to think they tripped and fell, so they don't make a peep. They spread their tails to help slow the descent.

One of the most common methods for keeping squirrels from climbing a feeder pole is the old "grease the pole" trick. This is not a good idea at all. It will actually kill the squirrel in cold weather. The grease

"You measured the bungee cords wrong, fuzz face!"

will mat his fur and cause him to die from hypothermia. Besides that, it isn't a long-term solution. The first few squirrels tend to wipe it off.

Hanging feeders, even dome-protected, are susceptible to squirrel attack. The problem with dome diners is that they do not take into account the lean, agile, athletic squirrels that can contort their bodies to extreme shapes. Most squirrels will hang precariously from the smallest piece of bark by one thin hair of the tail that has evolved over millions of years to hold the entire weight of a squirrel in a relaxed position for hours while eating.

Gnawty

Squirrels are gnawing animals, so if you ask them to stay off the birdfeeder they will always say, "Gnaw." They are tree dwellers. Their claws are suited for climbing, clinging, and swinging from trees, and also for seed grappling and feeder pole hugging.

The tail of a squirrel is used like a rudder. It helps give squirrels more direction in their lives and keeps them on the straight and narrow. A rodent's rudder is where these little furballs get their name. "Squirrel" comes from the Greek, meaning "shade-tailed."

The squirrel has two adze-shaped teeth above and below, with sharp edges suitable for chiseling into most birdfeeders on the market today. He uses his teeth like a can opener when working on a nut. He sometimes holds the nut and gnaws around it with his teeth, and sometimes he twirls the nut against his teeth. When using the first method, a squirrel always keeps his eyes closed so he doesn't get dizzy. If you ever watch one eating at your feeder, you will notice he not only keeps his eyes open, he also never blinks. This is because a squirrel's survival depends on constant eye contact with his unwilling benefactors. He will wait until the first signs of hostilities before he dashes away.

Osquirrelamosis

There is a very simple answer to squirrels gaining entrance to squirrel-proof feeders. The process is called "osquirrelamosis." This is the tendency of a squirrel to pass through a semipermeable membrane, like your feeder, into a concentrated space which then equalizes the feeding conditions on either side of the membrane.

This process is not fully understood by birdfeeder manufacturers at this time, so their claims of providing squirrel-proof birdfeeders are not quite dishonest. Of course, we can't overlook the fact that these devices don't work.

I am not trying to tell you squirrel-proof feeders are a waste of money because they do work on some squirrels. It is believed that some squirrels are not osmotic. Osmosis is a very complicated process, and many squirrels are just not mentally up to the task of physically performing the necessary osmotic steps that enable them to gain access to squirrel-proof feeders.

Your best defense is a good offense. Put out several nice squirrel feeders far away from the house if you do not want them hanging around harassing your birds. In most cases they will stay out and work the feeders that can be accessed without using the energy-draining osmosis procedure. But remember, when your squirrels are out of sight they are also out of minding distance.

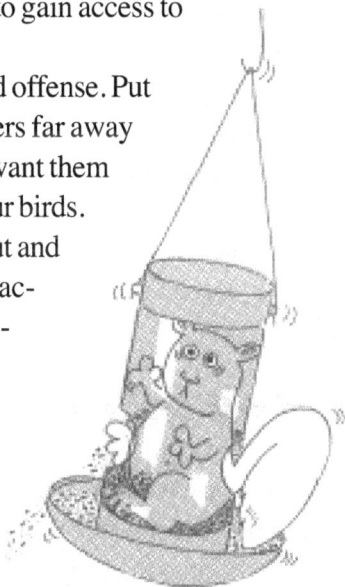

Par for the Course

I've seen squirrels upside down,
I've seen them downside up.
I've seen them swing by one toenail,
And drink from a coffee cup.
I've seen them jump a hundred yards,
And land on greasy poles.
I've seen them shinny down a wire,
And walk across hot coals.
I've watched them swim across a lake,
And dodge a speeding car.
But never have I seen a squirrel,
Shoot nine holes under par!   —DICKE. BIRD

Contrary to popular belief, the numbers of squirrels are declining. This is mostly due to loss of habitat. Squirrels seem more abundant because we continue to compress them into smaller living areas, as we have done with all of nature. Squirrels have become very adaptable to living close to people, even though they are quite often not welcomed with open arms. They used to run in herds, now they run when you are heard. We have taken away the heritage of the squirrel and made him a common beggar. He knows that what you put out is not for him. That has been made quite clear. When he climbs around all your fancy engineering and eats all your birdseed, he is trying to tell you he doesn't care what you think!

Flushed with Excitement

If asked how squirrels most often gain entry to a home, the majority of people would say down the chimney. Not so. I hate to make your bladder shy, but more squirrels enter houses through plumbing vent pipes than any other fashion. A squirrel often falls down the pipe and has no other option but to hold his nose, do a

124

little jockeying, Cousteau-style, and work his way into the commode. If you are sitting on the pot, it can be very exhilarating. The idea of this happening makes many people worry about their plumbing. Screening outside vents will help prevent this from happening. It will allow you to relax with confidence when reading your morning paper, knowing you will not be dethroned in the middle of the sports page by a cave-diving furball. So keep a lid on squirrel activity.

Toys

You cannot buy happiness, but some backyard birdfeeding enthusiasts try to bribe squirrels. Equipping your yard with squirrel feeders, various squirrel toys and athletic gear, only attracts more squirrels. If you wanted to keep the neighborhood kids out of your yard, would you build them a ballpark and install playground equipment? Why would anyone think that adding squirrel Ferris wheels, teeter-totters, and bungee cords would discourage furballs from spending time at birdfeeders? Exercise just makes them hungry. The reason these products have become so popular is not because they entertain squirrels, but because they entertain squirrel-watchers.

Magnetic Personalities

A squirrel is like a magnet to seed. A squirrel can physically jump twelve feet, but his magnetic personality will sometimes pull him another ten feet onto a birdfeeder. A squirrel always leads with his nose and comes out smelling like a rose. Being very success-oriented, squirrels have

cornered the market on cute. Most animals will steal your heart and then steal your food, but squirrels are more independent and self-assured. They take your seed and, as for your heart — they can take it or leave it.

The evolution of the birdfeeding industry has confused squirrels terribly. For years contraptions to keep furballs from gaining access to birdfeeders were big sellers. The demand grew for these products and more contraptions were marketed. Soon it dawned on the consumer that this was a vicious circle. The more you challenge a squirrel, the more his education will cost you. It is estimated that you can send your child to medical school cheaper than you can educate your squirrels to stay off the birdfeeder.

Sir Hairy Hillary
First Squirrel to Climb Mt. Greasepole

As squirrel education costs have skyrocketed, people have finally come to the conclusion that it would be cheaper just to feed the little

> **A fool and his birdseed are soon parted.**

furballs. It's funny how history seems to repeat itself. First, squirrels owned North America. Then Native Americans and Europeans cultivated it and grew fields of corn. To squirrels these were fields of dreams. But the cultivators cropped the competition by annihilating the squirrelly neighborhoods. Now, with the millions of dollars spent annually on squirrel feeders and toys, thousands of acres of corn are planted and harvested just to cater to suburban squirrels with an ear for corn. They don't even have to con corn out of most people with backyard feeders. Squirrels have come a long way, baby! Squirrels of the next century will be yard yuppies with expensive tastes and time to waste.

The "Look"

When it comes to competition for food at the feeder, the alpha squirrel is easy to spot by the "look." This furball never has to make a sound; all he has to do is supply the "look." The "look" can be felt. The dominant squirrel controls food flow. If another animal approaches the feeder, the dominant squirrel will shoot a "look" that would make a wood duck — duck. This will usually end the challenge. If not, a bluff charge is in order. If you study your squirrels, you will discover a whole arsenal of "looks."

There is the "straight-on look," the "side-shot look," the "short look," the "long look," the "glance dance," and the "glare stare."

Each "look" was developed for a particular situation, and some are used in combination with the "bluff charge." At the same time, optic nerves have to network with hearing capabilities. When a squirrel is concentrating on the "look," he still has to hear the side door of the house quietly open. He has to hear the bristles of the broom flutter in the still morning air. Some say a squirrel has the ability to hear the rapid heartbeat of a homeowner through double-pane glass. This is a myth. A squirrel has exceptional hearing, but it is not that good. What the squirrel detects through the window is — the "look."

The Hot Tongue and the Cold Shoulder

There are several brands of hot pepper powder to mix with birdseed that supposedly keeps squirrels out of your feeder and out of your life. These concoctions were originally developed for use in the poultry industry to control feed shrinkage by rats. Maybe this is where "hot and spicy" chicken comes from.

I was quoted in *The Wall Street Journal* as saying, "I tried it and seconds later I had three squirrels knocking at the door asking for a Dos Equis® beer." This is not so far from the truth. These products do not seem to bother my squirrels or raccoons. I was told by one company official that squirrels have to develop a distaste for the products. Now there's a new marketing twist I have never heard before! For the price of additives, you can buy additional seed and take your squirrels to lunch. I have to wonder what it might do to the digestive system of birds that eat it.

Another new technology in squirrel thwarting is battery-operated shock treatments. One feeder will give off a mild shock when the squirrel mounts it. The batteries in this feeder do not last very long, but the idea is that the squirrel doesn't know that, and he'll never come back to the feeder that bit him.

Squirrel-Proof

• PVC piping surface has proven to be a slippery and effective anti-squirrel device. It can be used as a mounting post or baffle.

• Stovepipe mounted on a metal pole with an enclosed upper end will act as an effective squirrel baffle.

• A Slinky® (a spring-coil toy), slid over the feeder pole and attached to the feeder, is a slick way to slink a stealthy seed-stealing squirrel.

• A $33^{1/3}$ rpm record tied above a hanging feeder works well as a baffle.

• Spring-loaded feeder poles will spook squirrels for about ten seconds.

• Clear plastic oxygen tubing, covering feeder support wire, creates a squirrel log roller.

• Old thread spools threaded on wire also works well for log rolling your squirrel.

• Yelling through a baby monitor taped to the feeder pole.

• Piped-in tape-recorded hawk sounds.
• Screw six-inch-wide Plexiglas® sheets to bottom edges of a pole-mounted feeder, creating a baffle.

• Baffles made from wash tubs, coffee cans, fruit tins, garbage can lids, or milk jugs.

• Custom feeders that screen out squirrels but have openings large enough for small songbirds to enter.

"We'll start with these three, then clear-cut the whole yard."

• *Olé* method. Tie a rope to the feeder. When the squirrel launches from a tree, pull the rope and quickly move the feeder.
• Thick thorn bushes wrapped tightly around the feeder pole. You will need a bulletproof vest to fill the feeder.

• Battery-operated remote-controlled model dune buggy.

• Cut the bottom off a plastic gallon bleach bottle and slip it onto the bird-feeder pole. This acts as a baffle and causes a "bottle-neck" for your squirrels.

• Ziploc® water wrath. Fill a sandwich bag half-full of water and lob it at your squirrel so that it opens on impact and cannot be thrown back.

Recap and Reinforce

• An above-feeder squirrel baffle will double as an umbrella for your seed dispenser, keeping your birdfood not only high but dry.

• Besides nuts and your birdseed, a squirrel will eat tree buds, bark (for sap), tree seeds, insects, birds' eggs, corn, fruit, spruce cones, mushrooms, acorns, and snails. A squirrel will eat anything that does not eat him first.

• Over 60 percent of the squirrels that are used to eating at birdfeeders would rather fight you than switch.

• Squirrels are born with a natural gift of grab.

• In the early 1800s migrating squirrels traveled in herds estimated to contain nearly a quarter-million animals. There are records of bands of squirrels advancing along fronts a hundred miles wide and requiring five days to pass. (And you think you have problems.)

• A squirrel uses his tail for communication, a fifth leg, a parachute, a blanket for warmth, a sunshade to stay cool, and an umbrella to keep dry.

• Relocated squirrels, on average, find their way home sooner than the re-locator.

• Squirrels can move their jaws faster than a blender on the liquid setting. They must stop chewing to listen for signs of danger.

• Squirrels do use smell and memory in searching for food. They smell sunflower seed and remember it is in your birdfeeder.

"We'll start with these three, then clear-cut the whole yard."

• Squirrels are live-born, not hatched from sunflower seeds as once theorized.

• Squirrels are not concerned with the controversy over whether the peanut is a nut, vegetable, seed, or butter. To them it is just an hors d'oeuvre.

• Chipmunks get their name from the Greek chip, meaning "fat," and munk, meaning "face."

• Squirrels have acute vision, acute hearing, and acute little face.

• Every squirrel-proof feeder design idea has a disadvantage equal to or exceeding the usufulness of the original idea.

• Flying squirrels can glide many yards on the thin fur-covered membranes between their front and rear legs. Baffles are useless in thwarting them.

• Squirrels do not always remember where they buried their nuts. Most suffer from "sometimers" disease.

• The farther up a tree a squirrel can climb, the farther he can leap. It is called the "leap of faith." He closes his eyes, jumps, and hopes with all his might that he hits his target.

• Baldness in squirrels is caused by skin parasites and maybe stress if you have been yelling at them. The cure is some whole wheat bread in flaxseed oil, dusted with brewer's yeast, and spread with a little peanut butter.

Dear Dick E. Bird

Dear Dick E. Bird

My husband has found a surefire method of keeping squirrels off the bird-feeders, but he is beginning to get on my nerves. I think he is possessed with his new squirrel game. I cannot get him to do anything around the house or go anywhere anymore. It's all my fault. I bought him a remote-controlled miniature dune buggy for Christmas and he uses it to chase squirrels all over the yard. He's like a kid with a new toy. Should I hide it from him or what?
—Frustrated in Frankfort

Dear Frustrated:

Don't hide the dune buggy. He will know you did it. Hide the squirrels! —Keep Smilin', Dick E. Bird

Dear Dick E.. Bird:

I don't mind feeding squirrels, but I have a red squirrel I call Vicious. He hogs the feeder, has a very bad temper, and eats the feed up in a matter of hours. I hope this is not genetic because I think he might be raising a family. How many offspring do red squirrels have a year? Will they all stay here with me?

—Fed Up in Fruitport

Dear Fed:

Red squirrels are known to be very mouthy. They are little squirrels and seem to have a chip on their shoulders. They will often have two litters a year if the food supply is adequate and it sounds like yours is. They will have three to seven young in every batch, so you could end up with six to fourteen new customers each year. Hawks and foxes will control your population to some degree, but you are still going to have a lot of little sons of Vicious running your yard very soon.

—Keep Smilin', Dick E. Bird

Tongue-in-Jowl Tidbits

If you think you now understand how a squirrel works, read this chapter again. You don't get it yet — squirrels cannot be reckoned with.

APPLY FUZZY FACTS

1. What do you call a squirrel's nest?
2. How can you tell if a squirrel has been in your birdfeeder?
3. Why will a moth never cry when eaten by a squirrel?
4. What does a squirrel do when you chase him off the birdfeeder with a broom?

DISCUSSION TOPICS

1. What is the difference between a squirrel and a terrorist?
2. What do you call a squirrel's habit of burying each nut separately?
3. How many squirrels does it take to knock a hole in a wooden birdfeeder?
4. What part of an automobile have studies shown kills most squirrels?

FURBALL TRIVIA

1. Will aftershave sprinkled around the birdfeeder keep squirrels off?
2. What does a squirrel use for warmth, balance, shade, and communications?
3. How fast can a squirrel run?
4. Why do squirrels produce two litters of young a year?
5. Squirrel cheeks are made of what natural material unique in the animal world?
6. What is the largest American tree squirrel?
7. What happens when a squirrel gets into your peanut butter?
8. Why do squirrels spend so much time in trees?

AND THE ANSWER IS—

Apply Fuzzy Facts: 1. Nutcracker Suite. 2. You can smell birdseed on his breath. 3. Because you can't make a moth bawl. 4. He yells, "Nuts!" and bolts. **Discussion Topics:** 1. You can negotiate with a terrorist. 2. Scatter-hoarding. 3. Three. One to hold the feeder and two to hold the woodpecker. 4. The nut directly behind the wheel. **Furball Trivia:** 1. No, but it will make them smell much better. 2. The tail. 3. 12 miles per hour with a tail wind. 4. For tax purposes. 5. Spandex. 6. Fox squirrel. 7. You get a squirrel that sticks to the roof of your mouth. 8. To get away from all the nuts on the ground.

*Habitat is not only removed
quietly from a generation of
man, but also from multiple
generations of wildlife, which
unknowingly adapt to less
and become distorted by a
change they never even feel.*
—DICK E. BIRD

5•

Look, Mom, No Cavities!

Birds Are the World's
Largest Quality Home Builders

Approximately fifty North American bird species will use a man-made nesting box. Building a nesting box for a bird is a lot more complicated than most people realize. One of the biggest mistakes "birdhouse builders" make is adding a perch at the entrance opening. I have never been able to find the historical source for that perch idea, but it is the worst addition you can add to a bird-house. It actually creates a perch for a predator to sit and harass and even kill the occupants of the nesting box. Cavity-nesting birds often use abandoned woodpecker nest sites and decaying tree cavities. If you were to explore some of these sites, you would notice none of them have a short piece of quarter-inch doweling attached directly beneath the opening. So don't put one on your birdhouse.

Trees do not need dentists because they have their cavities filled automatically by birds and other critters. A hollow tree cavity develops in two ways. The first is when part of the tree decays and gravity instructs it to cave in, creating a natural cavity. Woodpeckers are very impatient birds and will not wait for this process. Woodpeckers often abandon the cavities they have excavated, giving other birds a chance to get a rotten deal on a house.

Birds have certain needs and housing requirements. You must be a good real estate agent and buy or build the right home for the needs of the family of birds you wish to be your next-nest neighbors. I have seen people spend all winter building a bird palace and then never give a second thought to how or where it should be placed. Successfully attracting birds to a handmade habitat takes planning and common sense.

After you get the architectural problems solved and have the perfect Frank Lloyd Wright design that will attract the birds of choice, you have only made a good start. Location is your next important step. If your placement does not meet bird safety regulations, they will not move in no matter how gorgeous the house looks.

Placement Points to Ponder

• A good rule of thumb is not to place more than two or three nest boxes out per acre for any one species.

• Put about one hundred yards between bluebird boxes, and seventy-five yards between tree swallow boxes. If you have both species, they will not compete for the same food source, but they will compete for nesting space. One solution is to place a second nesting box several yards away and then leave a hundred-yard buffer to your next set of boxes. This will help alleviate any terrible turf wars. This is only a rule of thumb. I have many bluebird boxes much closer that enjoy almost 100 percent occupancy by bluebirds, tree swallows, and chickadees.

• Houses mounted on metal poles are less vulnerable to predators than houses attached to tree trunks or hanging from limbs.

• Putting more than one box in the same tree is not a good idea, but if you only have one tree, a choice might not be a bad idea. Seldom will more than one box be utilized for nesting, although many will be used for branch offices and dummy nests.

• If you anticipate hot weather, face the entrance holes north or east to help minimize overheating.

> *Never look a swift bird in the mouth.*

• Do not erect birdhouses near feeders or baths. Birds are very secretive nesters, and constant activity around feed stations and baths will discourage nesting in the vicinity.

Keep the Ceiling Waterproof and the Floor Leaky: Construction, Mounting, and Problem-Solving Tips

• Make sure you have provided drain holes to let excess water seep away. Birds love being wild, but they don't want to be wet and wild.

• Make sure you have provided ventilation and used a material that insulates the nesting bird from the summer's heat (three-quarter-inch wood stock). Drill several half-inch holes near the top of the birdhouse to promote good ventilation. It can get egg-stremely uncomfortable setting on your kids in close quarters on a sunny day.

• Do not put perches on any nesting boxes. It is only a place for predators to sit and harass the rightful tenant. Birds can enter a hole without any problem. They have been practicing entering natural nonperched hollow trees for eons. Roughen the areas below the entrance hole or cut several kerfs for birds to use for clinging. Do the same on the inside so that the little eggheads can have a toehold to climb out when they are ready to face reality.

The Birdhouse

They always like them high and dry,
Unfurnished and real plain.
They like a hole of proper size,
Protected from the rain.
They like some drainage in the floor,
Some air space in the ceiling.
Sitting in a soggy nest,
Gives them a sinking feeling.   —DICK E. BIRD

• Have the roof extend out three or four inches. This will protect the entrance from the elements and extend predator reach. It will also create some shade.

• Do not use wood treated with preservative. Most lumber yards sell it and the copper-based preservative has become a popular home building material. When exposed to water, this treatment can produce poisonous vapors that are harmful to birds in a confined area.

140

• Think about how you're going to mount the nesting box as you design it. Many people never give this a thought until their prize nesting box is ready to go and they find they forgot to leave room to secure them with fasteners.

• Look closely at the nails you are going to use. Galvanized make a good choice, but they tend to loosen over time. Another choice would be brass shank nails. Always "toe-nail" your houses together (by driving the nails into your masterpiece at a slant). Use screws if at all possible. Make sure you can tell the difference between a good galvanized nail and the one on the end of your thumb.

"Ernie, I think the purple Martians are back."

• Birdhouses tend to get messy, so when your tenants leave, you have to go out and clean it out. That's why you want your birdhouse to open. Use screw eyes wherever you have to secure an opening. Better than a latch or loose nail, a screw eye will secure the nesting box shut and it will not be accidentally knocked open by a raccoon or other predator. By using a screw eye, you can open the box — to monitor and clean — by easily twisting the eye.

• Use thick wood, as it provides for better insulation.

Backward Glances

They stand their ground,
And sing their song,
They let you have a look;
You note their color,
Voice, and form,
But they're never in the book.
Maybe it's my book of birds,
There's something that it lacks;
Perhaps I need another one,
That shows birds from the back.
I don't always hear them,
When they make their sounds;
And I can never get those birds,
To stop and turn around.   —DICK E. BIRD

• Never use screw eyes to hang a nesting box. Use an eyebolt and a locking nut. The screw eye will work its way out and the box will end up on the ground.

• The secret to a safe birdhouse design is extending the reach of the hole against potential predators. Many nesting boxes are designed with hole extensions. Another way to extend the reach is to widen the roof overhang. In most cases, the predator will sit on top of the box where it is comfortable, and try to reach down into the box for its prize. A wide roof or a piece of shingle nailed to the top of the box will help discourage this action.

• The areas that are cleared for rights-of-ways make excellent nesting box locations because they are open fields bounded by trees. Before you mount nesting boxes on utility poles, you should check with the utility company involved. After several years of mounting boxes on utility poles in my area, my local power provider informed me that nesting boxes could not be placed on any of their poles — transformer or not. I had to take my name off every one of those boxes!

• Design the floor of your birdhouse within the sidewalls so that water is funneled directly off the bottom of the nesting box.

• Metal or wood purple martin houses have proven to be equally adequate. They seem to perform about the same under temperature testing. The wood models are self-insulating and the metal models are coated in light colors that reflect heat.

• The box opening should hinge down for the best access in cleaning and viewing.

• The entry hole should meet specifications recommended for the species you are trying to attract.

• Tenants — mice and flying squirrels — will use nesting boxes if you leave them closed during the winter. To prevent this, leave your nesting boxes hinged open. Besides tenants, you might find your nesting boxes being used for storage during the winter. I have found them stuffed with mushrooms, acorns, and berries.

NESTING BOX DIMENSION CHART

Species	Floor	Depth	Entrance height above floor	Entrance hole diameter	Suggested mounting Height
Nuthatch	4 x 4 in.	8-10 in.	6-8 in.	1¼ in.	12-20 ft.
Most wrens	4 x 4 in.	6-8 in.	4-6 in.	1-1½ in.	6-10 ft.
Chickadee	4 x 4 in.	8-10 in.	6-8 in.	1¼ in.	6-15 ft.
Tree swallow	5 x 5 in.	6 in.	1-6 in.	1½ in.	5-15 ft.
Bluebird	5 x 5 in.	8 in.	6 in.	1½ in.	3-6 ft.
Purple martin*	6 x 6 in.	6 in.	1 in.	2½ in.	15-20 ft.
Flycatcher	6 x 6 in.	8-10 in.	6-8 in.	2 in.	8-20 ft.
House finch	6 x 6 in.	6 in.	4 in.	2 in.	8-13 ft.
Woodpecker (S)	4 x 4 in.	8-10 in.	6-8 in.	1¼ in.	7-20 ft.
Woodpecker (M)	6 x 6 in.	12-16 in.	9-12 in.	2 in.	12-20 ft.
Flicker	7 x 7 in.	16-19 in.	14-16 in.	2½ in.	7-20 ft.
Robin[1]					
Phoebe[1]					

*Purple martins are colony nesters. This dimension is one compartment of at least eight.

[1]Robin and phoebe nesting shelves should be roughly 5 x 7 in. and at least 8 feet off the ground.

You have to take all of these dimensions with a grain of salt on a bird's tail. Forty percent of my bluebird houses end up being occupied by chickadees. Wrens will nest in just about anything, and flickers are tough to attract no matter what you do. Unless you see a bird flitting around with a tape measure in his tool belt, expect to find various birds in nesting boxes you have designed for a specific species. Use this chart as a guideline. Monitoring your efforts will give you direction for how much adjustment to make for optimum results.

• To discourage wasps, rub soap on the inside roof of the box where they would begin attaching a nest.

• You should never put all your eggs in one basket, so install several nesting boxes. Remember, the birds have never read this book and they do not always know how to act. A well-designed bluebird house will attract several species of birds that are not supposed to care for the cavity size, opening, or location.

• Several nesting boxes constitute a "trail." Making the rounds to check the boxes on your "trail" can be very rewarding.

• If you paint or stain a nesting box, do not coat the interior.

• Glue each joint for strength.

I always figured the popular Peterson Bluebird House had a guy named Peterson behind it, so I decided to find him and ask him how he came to be the father of this very successful birdhouse design. Dick Peterson was a hunter and a trapper, a man of the out-of-doors. When he set his mind to helping rebuild the bluebird populations in his area, he first called the Audubon Society in New York for a set of box plans. Dick built some of these boxes, but found that they were less than satisfactory to the birds. So he did just what he tells people to do today: "Watch the bluebirds and they will tell you what they need."

Dick used his common sense and his knowledge of birds to design a more functional nesting box for the bluebird. He figured the box did not have to be conventionally square, since natural tree cavities chipped out by woodpeckers have round bottoms. He also noticed the adults having to duck to feed the young as they grew and begged at the opening. He experimented with the elongated hole design and found it offered the adults some pivot

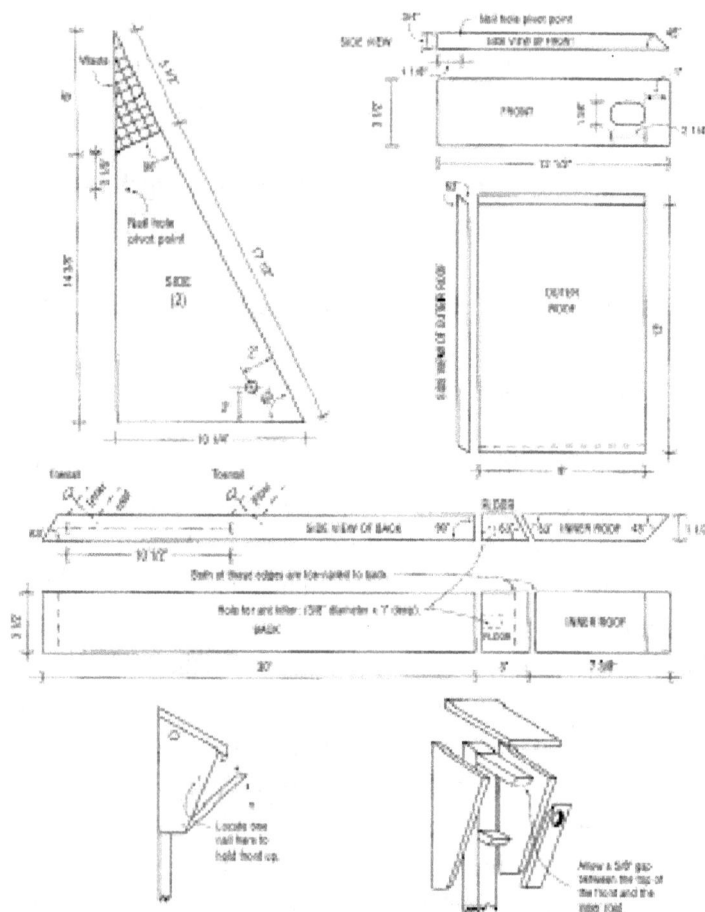

Peterson design

room when feeding into the box.

Little by little, he narrowed the box opening, until the starlings stopped using it, but the bluebirds continued.

The Peterson design is distributed by Minnesota Nongame Wildlife. Their book *Woodworking for Wildlife* is the best resource available for nesting box plans and the royalties go to providing nongame wildlife funding. As the state nongame wildlife program supervisor of Minnesota in the late 1970s, Carrol L. Henderson saw the need to bring together the widely scattered and frequently incorrect information that was available about bird nesting boxes. He contacted the persons that he considered to be the nation's best experts on various species and asked for their specific recommendations on how to attract them, including nesting box specifications. Then he took those designs and collaborated with Northwest Airlines pilot (and avid amateur carpenter) Dave Ahlgren, and asked him what was wrong with these biologists' designs from the standpoint of an amateur wood-worker. Together they eliminated as many odd-angled cuts as possible and developed many one-board birdhouse designs that could quickly and easily be cut out and assembled by bird enthusiasts with limited woodworking ability and simple tools.

> *"The strength of a nation lies in the homes of its birds."*
> —Abraham Larkin

The impact of the Civil War is not over yet. Frank Zuern of Oshkosh, Wisconsin, on a visit to Chickamauga, Georgia, in 1980, noticed a bluebird nesting in the bore of a Civil War cannon. That chance encounter led Frank to design a new-style bluebird nesting box. The Tree Branch Bluebird House is not only desirable to bluebirds but also to chickadees and tree swallows. Predators that eat eggs and young are the biggest problem in running a successful nesting box trail system. Zuern's design extends the reach to eliminate this problem. He says the design copies what nature

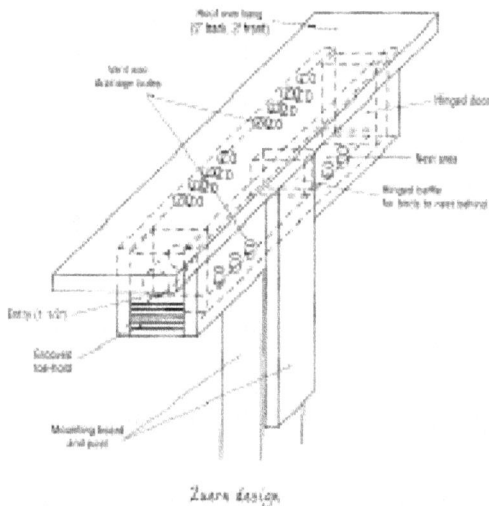

Zaara design.

provided the birds for years — a broken hollow tree branch. House sparrows must be controlled for this nest box to be effective in bluebird restoration.

Those of you who do not know how to use power tools or have already cut off several important fingers will be in the market for commercially manufactured nesting boxes. Consumer awareness is perhaps the best method to improve product. Commercial nesting box construction has improved tremendously as the customer has become more educated on the needs of the species they plan to attract.

When shopping for a new home for your birds, be very careful that a slick salesperson doesn't sell you "oceanfront property in Arizona" or, worse yet, a nesting box for a bird that doesn't use a cavity. There are only about fifty birds in North America that will be attracted to a man-made nesting cavity. Do not expect to attract some of your favorite species, such as cardinals, goldfinches, and orioles, to a nesting box. You will only attract birds that are historically cavity nesters.

Plant life will play a very important role in attracting birds to a nesting box. Plants in your yard provide food, shelter, and perching areas for nesting birds. When choosing a nesting box, birds will consider the convenience and safety of surrounding vegetation. If you plant little trees next to your own house, they will grow into giant redwoods in four years, rot your shingles, and fall on the house after the first windstorm. If you plant small trees out on the lawn away from the house, they will never reach the height of your kneecap and you will have to mow around them for the next decade. Plan your plantings carefully to benefit wildlife and your viewing of them.

Habitat

Loss of nesting habitat is one of the major reasons bird populations are in decline and one of the reasons nesting box construction is growing in popularity. Boy Scouts, church groups, senior citizen organizations, schoolchildren, and thousands of individuals working in the garage where their spouses sent them, are building nesting boxes for all types of birds they wish to attract. Many of these groups also monitor nesting box trails to ensure boxes have the best opportunity to be occupied and not destroyed by predators. There was a time when almost any structure put up would be used by birds as a nesting cavity. Those times have changed as the number of birds has decreased. It is more important now than ever to offer bird housing that imitates the natural need of the

"This is a nice tree-bedroom that could fit your needs."

species desired.

To maximize the chance of successful occupancy, you need to follow some simple management practices: Proper design, location, and monitoring will boost your ratio of active units.

Detailed information is available at most well-stocked libraries. Hole size, inside dimension, height location, materials, ventilation requirements, drainage, predator guards, approach, and timing are all considerations. Take some time to

"I think they're supposed to be four hundred yards apart, Ernie, not four hundred per yard."

not only build some nesting boxes but to do it right. This way you will get to know something about the new neighbors you hope to attract.

Cleaning

Do not end up being a slumlord—keep boxes maintained and cleaned. Cleaning nesting boxes, after birds have fledged, is important and gives the box a better chance of being used for second and third broods. Clean the boxes at the end of the nesting season and check them in the early spring in preparation for the coming nesting season.

You will appreciate the convenience of a nesting box design that allows the viewing wall to swing out and down when you begin to clean. The same principle, that allows easy viewing, allows easy cleaning of hard-to-reach corners.

Many people use a mild solution of bleach to clean feeders and boxes. One capful of bleach per gallon is more than enough. Nonpolluting biodegradable bleach that contains no phosphates or chlorine is also available. Another surefire method is scorching the inside of the box with a small butane soldering torch.

Build Them and They Will Come

One of the most satisfying projects around the house is building a birdhouse and having the intended actually move into it. Birds can sometimes be very choosy.

They will often inspect and pass up a nice-looking nesting box. The ultimate "slap in the face" is when they simply ignore your work of art. You spend hours designing a box just right for them, and they nest nearby in a hollow stump. Do not take it personally. I have had birds nest on top of my boxes. I could have saved a lot of money by just building a roof.

If you provide the proper nesting box structures and place them securely, birds should flock to them. But the salesperson in you might want to help push a particular model or location. To attract bluebirds to boxes, I often place currants on the roof in the spring. I stick them on the carpet tack strips I nail to the roof. The purpose for the carpet tack strips is to make fat cats (and raccoons), that decide to sit on the roof and harass my birds, uncomfortable.

Putting up several boxes in various locations will enable you to pinpoint which locations are the most popular within just a few years. Once a box in a certain location has produced fledglings, it is almost a sure bet it will be used again and again, year after year.

Grow Your Own

You can grow some very durable housing for your birds if you have a green thumb and some black dirt. All you will need are some Lagenarias gourd seeds, sunshine, and water. These are the hard-shelled variety of gourd that will last for years after they are cured. When harvested, the gourds are 90 percent water. Wash them real well and store them in a dry place. Let them dry for three or four months. You can tell by their light weight and brown woody exterior when they are cured. After drilling an entrance hole, shake out as much dry material as possible and save the seeds for your next crop. Drill some drainage holes in the bottom and wire hanging holes in the top. You will have to clean these nesting cavities through the 2½-inch entrance hole. Use your fingers, but don't bite your tongue.

Recap and Reinforce

• Hang out a wire cage full of construction materials for nesting birds — for example, animal hair, wool, feathers, or very short pieces of string or twine.

• Mount feeders on metal poles for the best chances of outwitting predators.

• Create a "mud puddle" to offer swallows, robins, and other birds a bathing and nesting material pit stop.

• Horizontal slots instead of circular openings on nesting boxes will sometimes make them more attractive to uncoordinated birds that can never seem to get those long, crooked sticks through small, round holes.

• Offering birds such as robins and phoebes a nesting shelf will help locate them and their droppings away from traffic areas around the house.

• There is no such thing as "one size fits all" when it comes to bird housing construction. Custom-built nesting boxes fit the needs of various species. Find out whom you want for neighbors and what they want from you.

• An excellent building material is three-quarter-inch cedar. It is long-lasting, has good insulating qualities, and breathes.

• Dull coloring reflects heat and is less likely to draw predators.

• Gourds make excellent bird housing, and they were possibly the first man-made birdhouses. Native Americans used gourds to attract birds.

• Without ventilation, nesting boxes can turn deadly in extreme heat. Leave gaps in the floor and the upper sides of boxes or drill several quarter-inch holes at both locations.

• Drilling the entrance hole at an upward angle can help prevent water going into the box during a driving rain.

• Clean the boxes after each brood fledges. Many birds will not nest again in a box full of old nesting material. If you clean out your box, the birds will likely use the same box for two or three broods a season.

• Leaving a nesting box opened during the winter will eliminate its being used as a mouse house. If closed up, they could become shelters for winter birds and squirrels, which you may want to attract.

• Angling the roof on a nesting box will shed moisture and discourage predators from sitting on top of the nesting box and harassing the occupants.

• Identify the birds that are most likely to be attracted to the habitat your property offers and then put the appropriate nesting box in the right place to welcome them in.

• When building a birdhouse, don't cut corners or fingers.

Dear Dick E. Bird

Dear Dick E. Bird:

I think I have been swindled. My wife said I was sitting around too much after retiring, so I decided to get into real estate. I bought a birdhouse at a craft show with a suet holder on the side. The crafter said I could not only house my birds but feed them too. The birds do eat from the suet, but how can I get them to nest in the house?

—Room and Bored in Bad River

Dear Bored:

This is not good. Actually, you do not have a big problem. Just split the two up. Take the suet feeder off the house and nail it to one of your birdfeeders. You certainly wouldn't want all your neighbors down at your place eating all day while you were trying to raise a family—and neither do your birds. There are products that can be used for a feeder or a house but never both at the same time. You have to make up your mind. Either feed 'em or breed 'em.

—Keep Smilin', Dick E. Bird

Dear Dick E. Bird

We have been watching a mama bird in our yard moving her eggs and fooling with them constantly. What is her problem?

—Egging 'em on in Evergreen

Dear Egg:

This is called an egg roll. You have probably heard people say many times, "I'll have my eggs over easy." Well, this is exactly how mama feels. She turns her eggs several times a day so that the embryos develop properly. You will usually see her or her mate turning the eggs with their bills. Don't worry, when they hatch, those little birdbrains come out sunny-side up every time, and I guarantee, there is not an egghead among them.

—Keep Smilin', Dick E. Bird

Tongue-in-Beak-Tidbits

If you have gleaned some constructive material from this chapter, move on to the next. Any area you feel needs more work can be nailed down at a later date.

APPLY FEATHERED FACTS

1. What flies, dives, swoops, and eats thousands of mosquitoes a night?
2. How do robins handle their feeding responsibilities?
3. What fish is named after the dumbest thing you can put on a birdhouse?
4. Where is the most productive place to locate a birdhouse?

DISCUSSION TOPICS

1. What is the best rule of thumb when sawing out nesting box parts?
2. When will cavity-nesting birds be ground nesters?
3. How big should the entrance hole on a birdhouse be?
4. How many entrances should a birdhouse have?

BIRD-BRAINED TRIVIA

1. What was likely the first nesting cavity offered to birds by man?
2. What is the best thing about building a birdhouse?
3. Why should you leave your nesting boxes up all winter?
4. Why do some birds nest on the ground?
5. What pesticide is blamed for causing bird eggs to thin and fail to hatch?
6. What is a birdhouse?
7. What do birds look for when checking out a birdhouse to check into?
8. What is the first thing young birds are taught before leaving the nesting box?

AND THE ANSWER IS—

Apply Feathered Facts: 1. A bat. 2. They worm their way out of them. 3. A perch. 4. Outdoors. **Discussion Topics:** 1. Keeping it attached to your hand. 2. When you don't secure the nesting box properly. 3. Bigger than the bird. 4. One entrance and one exit, but they should both be the same hole. **Bird-Brained Trivia:** 1. A gourd. 2. No building inspector. 3. Some birds will use them for roosting boxes. 4. They are afraid of heights. 5. DDT. 6. Man's effort to improve his lot. 7. A room with a view. 8. Straighten up and fly right.

Civilization is the adaptation of a large group of people to the physical environment. Ecology is one of the considerations that makes the adaptation successful.
—DICKE. BIRD

6•
Seeds of Thought

Connection

Human beings are inextricably connected to birds. Birds have played an important part in every part of our history. They have been woven into our lives through religion, philosophy, song, dance, medicine, dress, poetry, science, folklore, myth, superstition, art, and even weather forecasting—everything that tends to make us civilized. Why have we relegated so much importance to birds, yet treat them with such little respect? As we begin to lose bird species, we will also lose portions of our heritage that we share with the birds.

We have used birds for everything from medicinal purposes to hat dressings. Miners used to use canaries to detect deadly gas in their working environments. The popularity of birds today and the impressive growth in the birdfeeding industry are most likely explained by the fact that birds are our most accessible wildlife.

Attracting birds and observing them is not a new concept. Long before our celebrated naturalists and artists began to record species and habit, early man recognized birds for their numerous benefits. We know that various wanderers of time recorded birds in carved stone and pictograph collages. It is incredible to think that an ancient artisan, sitting on a hillside thousands of years ago, might have been doing the same thing many of us still enjoy today — watching birds, studying them, and marveling at the abilities they possess.

It doesn't matter how long you have enjoyed watching birds at the feeder; there is always something new going on. Once you get to know the players, you begin to understand the social pattern of the various feed stations. You see who is most dominant and how the others deal with it. You find that every bird is an individual and that they all lead very hectic lives. It takes a lot of energy to keep a flying machine in tip-top condition. Every seed you put out for your birds is quickly turned into a burst of energy (and a bird dropping). Birds must work hard from sunup to sundown to maintain their fragile existence.

If you watch your birds reacting to one another at the feeder, you can see that life is a series of skirmishes. Boundaries are set and broken, territories are breached and reestablished, dialogue is volleyed continuously, and action is often swift and violent. Size and strength are important, but shrewdness often determines the winner in a conflict. Might is often checked with wit, and aggression with withdrawal. The scenario seldom changes as each new generation of birds comes to the feeder — only the players do. Birds will quickly learn the ramifications of these skirmishes if they plan to survive long at the perch. Resources are fought over, even in these small theaters of life, and the conqueror is always weary, always temporary.

Feeding birds will not save a single species from falling off the face of the Earth. What it might do is make enough of us aware of the magic that is all around us, and help us see a much more diverse system of life that must be maintained.

Birds have become the most important factor in wildlife conservation. From an aesthetic point of view, a backyard without birds is a semidesert.

The interest millions of people are showing in birds has lead to education and understanding of the many natural communities and how they are linked. Birds are one of our most important indicator species; they are easy to attract and they are found almost everywhere on the globe.

Do not think that when you put out birdseed, you are making an environmental contribution. The birds that show up at your feeders are your return on a seed investment.

Our wild bird populations are declining faster now than at any other time in recorded history. I will be the first to agree that we cannot buy our way out of environmental concern, but we may be able to buy some time if we understand what our birds need.

Those drawn to birdfeeding will discover a connection to the broader issues that must be confronted when dealing with the rest of our natural world.

I believe the growth in birdfeeding is a direct result of a lack of connection with nature. The world has become a very busy place full of forced choices. Even though we think we are making our own decisions, we are more like cattle being prodded along and pushed into the many chutes of society. Not only is the tranquillity of nature becoming more difficult to find, so is time to look for that tranquillity.

"If you want more than three items, you will have to go to register five."

Feeding birds offers an excellent opportunity to stop and appreciate a very common and approachable part of nature.

When people first develop an interest and jump on the birdfeeding bandwagon, they experience a roller-coaster ride of feelings. They are attracted first to the diversity, color, and song of birds. Then they are overwhelmed by the simple facts and amazing oddities of birds that have been sitting right outside their windows for years. Soon they begin to realize just how important birds are to a healthy environment, how intricately they are bound and threaded in Earth's fabric. That's when the analogy of birds being the environmental barometer starts to make sense to them.

Watching birds is like hunting, only you are collecting snapshots of nature instead of meals. Bird life is so varied that there is never a dull moment. There is always something new and different at the backyard birdfeeder. You can watch birds anywhere and at any time of the year. All you need is some birdseed and a good pair of field glasses.

There is great value in the companionship of birds. There is a comfort in their presence, a mystery in their habits, and a sense of wonder in their colors and songs. The language between man and nature begins with birdsongs. Our attraction to birds is a natural one.

But man is becoming disassociated with his natural surroundings. At the same time, we are noticing the deterioration of bird populations. It is also interesting to note that the more we distance ourselves from nature, the stronger is our urge to reconnect with it. In the race to make more room for ourselves, dwindling wildlife habitat has become painfully apparent. For many of us, nature is as close as the backyard. The fact that feeding and viewing birds has become the fastest-growing hobby in North America, second in popularity only to gardening, says something about our inner desire to connect with nature.

The greatest thing about birds is variety. I have seen buzzards so large I mistook them for mountain sheep at a distance, and I have seen hummingbirds so small I thought at first glance they were insects. Birds come in every color of the rainbow, and each one is an individual. They not only vary in size and color but in shape and capabilities. Many times their shape has evolved to fit their capability, or was it their capability evolved to fit their shape? It doesn't matter. What matters is that they are very adaptable. But we are pushing them to a point where they cannot adjust fast enough anymore. We see the breakdown in more and more species each year. Birds and other wildlife are becoming exhausted by the pace and circumstances that we expect them to adapt to. Variety truly is the spice of life when it comes to birds, and we cannot afford to lose one more species.

Just as we have tamed and domesticated animals for a purpose to serve man, we have also tamed and domesticated our environment. We will eventually remove a whole generation from any heartfelt connection to the complexities of the natural world that surrounds them.

Relaxative

There is a huge culturally deprived segment of society that has no idea what bird-feeding is all about. Many of these people think they are too busy to feed birds. They don't want another responsibility. But actually, birdfeeding is a relaxative. It helps you loosen up, especially when you see the seed bill.

Feeding birds lets you turn off your lights for a while, park your brain, and idle your engine. Some people never get the opportunity to feed birds. Some are never exposed to the joy associated with watching colorful birds pick their pockets.

Those people who pass out cracked corn , who are economically stressed, and can't afford to buy quality seed for their birds, should be covered by a governmental surplus program so their birds can be grainfully deployed. It takes so little to do so much for so many.

Feeding birds is not the hassle some like to make it sound. Squirrels are the biggest complaint by far, but when you listen carefully, most of that dialogue sounds more like bragging. "Oh, yeah, well, my squirrel can jump forty feet from the pine tree to the perch." Some people love to hate their squirrels; others hate to leave their squirrels.

> *In a mad world nature is sanity's only hope.*

Even with the small headaches that go along with birdfeeding, you have to admit that many of the most memorable times in your life have called for an Excedrin ®. Squirrels can sometimes turn into a double-tablet-a-day habit, but this addiction can be curbed by simply adding a few squirrel feeders.

The world is not a perfect place, and birdfeeding can cause social problems if it turns compulsive. Compassion can turn ugly, even in the feeding of birds. If compulsion is not controlled, it can become all consuming, causing conflicts and creating catastrophic consequences.

Where Did They Go?

Bird migrations seem to have attracted the attention of man ever since he learned how to rub two sticks together. He would watch birds gather, then disappear in the autumn and return when the weather brought forth life once again in the spring. It was an annual cycle that impressed primitive man to such an extent that he regarded some birds as supernatural.

Like most subjects we humans debate, bird migration has had its share of theories. Some made sense and others were born of early crackpottery.

Early man was quick to notice that when the winter rush was on, most winged wonders headed south. Back then few cavemen

163

could afford to winter in the Sunbelt, and they had no idea there was a warmer place to spend the winter than next to a fire with a bunch of other semihibernating nonbathers. To pass the time, they would make up stories and most of these stories explained where the birds went every winter. Some believed that in the fall swallows would cling together, binding themselves into a feathered mass, and bury themselves in the mud with the frogs. Others thought the birds hibernated but not underwater, that they all congregated in bat caves and slept through the winter with the bats. One of my favorites is the "Everyone's Gone to the Moon" theory. Someone even wrote a song about it. About three hundred years ago scientists thought birds migrated to the moon for the winter and returned in the spring.

Aristotle was the first guy to take a scientific crack at the subject. "All animals have an instinctive perception of the changes of temperature, and just as men seek shelter in houses in winter, all animals that can do so shift their habitat at various seasons."

Now, before you go thinking Aristotle was a man ahead of his time, let me lay a few more of his theories on you. He thought the robin transformed itself into a redstart for the winter, and swallows would shed their feathers and hide out for that period of time. He put birds into three categories: migrants, hibernators, and transformers.

The moon theory came from some joker who didn't believe in the idea of migration and thought he would start an outrageous rumor to ridicule those who did. He said the trip to the moon took the birds over two months and that the birds would live off their fatty reserves during this travel time.

One enterprising young scientist joined the migrationist party after convincing himself that the hibernation theory was not sound. He put several swallows inside his icebox, where, despite the cold and the bad environment, the birds made no attempt to hibernate and promptly died.

Eventually, the migrationists won out and all the crazy stories those unbathed cavemen started years ago were put to rest, or hibernation at least!

Birdens

Birds lead very hectic lives. Besides adapting to the constant change that goes on around them, they face a lot of decision making. It can make a normal bird migrate in circles.

When they aren't roosting or flocking, they have to set up their territory, defend it against intruders, be sociable to nearby neighbors, and at the same time look carefully over the flock for a suitable mate. There is flight maintenance—constant preening to keep fit and trim and to ensure top soaring form. This preening schedule must work around foraging, storing, eating, and drinking. Besides the obvious bathing, there are dusting, anting, sunning, and molting. Most birds do not have time for complicated relationships. Courtship rituals must be followed, of course, but time cannot be wasted. There are nests to be built and defended, eggs to lay, incubation schedules to follow, parasites to be dealt with, fledglings to feed, and flying lessons to be given. The weather does not always cooperate, and many times a housing development is gobbling up the habitat right under them.

Communication skills are very important in the bird world. Birds continually work on fine-tuning their visual, vocal, and sexual communication skills. Young birds especially have to spend hours on singing lessons, mimicry, local and long-distance calls, and call forwarding. On top of everything else, they have to be alert at all times and on the lookout for scavengers, pirates, looters, and common thugs who would love to have them for dinner. Much time must be spent on watching their diet. There is plenty of pesticide-contaminated food going around these days, so a bird can't just eat and run. Time must be spent examining vegetable and insect matter because you are what you eat—

"I'm sorry, we can't afford any more seed until our Social Security check arrives."

and you aren't if you eat the wrong thing.

Birds have adapted very well over the centuries to secure for themselves a niche for survival. But the world is spinning much faster now; life has become much more complicated. Survival is a scramble. If all this sounds vaguely familiar, you should be as worried as I am!

Greased Lightning

A question many people have been asking themselves is: "Are my chances of being hit by lightning lesser or greater than being hit by bird droppings?"

There are many things to consider when trying to answer this question. First, there are many more birds than lightning bolts. When you hear thunder, you know you were not hit by lightning. If you hear a bird, however, it does not necessarily mean you weren't hit by a dropping. Your chances of getting hit by lightning used to be one in a million. But since the world population has increased, lightning has more targets, which makes your chances of getting hit by a bolt one in five million.

The same thing is true with birds. More people, more targets, less chance of being dropped on. Also, the world's bird populations are dropping dramatically, which makes getting hit with bird droppings even more rare.

But if you assume you will be hit by lightning, before you will be hit by a bird dropping, you are wrong. A weather system will only produce a small number of storms, and a storm will only produce a small number of lightning bolts, but birds will produce droppings continuously because birds have no bladders. Your actual chances of getting hit by a bird dropping is 150 percent.

Kid's Stuff

Progress with a better relationship towards our natural world can begin with a birdfeeder for your children outside the window of your home. The birds at our feeders should be our constant reminder of how small our world is. Many of the birds that live in your yard spend half their lives in other parts of the world. It might be our children's generation who will answer the questions we have so far elected to ignore.

Let your children find the secrets that songbirds possess. The discoveries to be made with the birds that visit daily will amaze and amuse. They will raise awareness and questions that will lead to understanding. If your kids or grandkids haven't had the chance to feed birds, they are missing a great deal. If you get them started, they will not only gain from observing birds but also get their first lesson in physics, watching squirrels get to the feeder. The potential for learning is incredible.

Do Birds Belch?

How many times have you sat at the window, watching your birds at the feeder, and wondered about this? Have you ever heard a bird burp? You would think birds would burp by the way they gulp down food.

The definition of a bird belch is "to eject [gas] noisily from the stomach through the beak." In France, if a bird belches at the birdfeeder it means it truly enjoyed the meal.

Compaction

By compacting our wildlife into smaller and smaller areas, we disrupt the breeding patterns that once occurred. Most of these changes are subtle. They are difficult to understand from numbers and data. You can only see and hear them if you have witnessed their passage. They are felt on many walks through a field spanning a lifetime.

> *It is un-American not to feed birds.*

The debate over world resources can be seen as several families living in one house and fighting over groceries. The house has three bedrooms and is comfortably designed for a family of four. There are only enough groceries to feed one family for a year. One family has a black Lab and a Siamese cat. Another family has elderly parents with a rare sense of humor. Another family has no kids, pets, or parents and just wants peace and quiet. One family has six kids and they are all party animals. Each family has to try to live together in the same house, but the groceries are going fast.

Each family will try to make their own case for cooperating and rationing groceries, but one thing is for sure: No one is going to survive if someone doesn't get off his duff and start cultivating a garden. The same goes for our resources.

> **We must live our reverence for nature in order to share it with others.**

It is often easier to celebrate nature's sounds, sights, and sensations and ignore the imbalance that hangs over this intricate web. But we must deal with the loss, the compromises, and the ever-growing resource demands. Every day, man moves farther away from a daily relationship with his own natural environment. We all become more and more like the kid who thinks the stork brings the baby. A true understanding of nature is lost in the distribution and packaging of resources brought to our doorstep.

This distancing creates a false sense of control over the environment. We have created a gulf between understanding the need for biodiversity and actually doing something to help us retain that biodiversity. The farther we distance ourselves from the basics of life, the more vulnerable we become.

Bird migration is an example of our borderless world. We build fences, but we cannot keep birds from flying over them. In simpler times it was felt the world and its elements could be controlled. Even though we know this is not possible, we have yet to admit it. Our everyday living habits now have a global effect. The birds that don't return in the spring are bad news. Each year we experience another degree of silence. Nature's scope is so vast that we have a tough time gauging its condition and a tougher time convincing ourselves of the realities around us. To obtain a wiser reading, we must look at a larger time frame than our own life span. We must make resource decisions based on facts of yesterday and the needs of tomorrow, not just the demands of today. We must not let our birds become extinct by denying their rights to adequate resources and pure elements that we all require to survive.

Are the Earth's Natural Resources Infinite or Exhaustible?

I believe the Earth's natural resources are both. They are infinite in a miraculous way, but at the present time they are exhausted. You can take the word "exhausted" to mean "depleted" or "just worn out." We all know that life-forms have limitations. Example: passenger pigeons were one of the most successful breeding species in history. They numbered in the billions. But after we market-hunted them into small fragmented populations, they lost their natural ability to breed and became extinct.

Our sun seems to guarantee us at least another five hundred billion years of life-giving light. So maybe all the Earth needs is a rest, a period of recuperation — voluntarily, before total exhaustion will be forced upon us.

Vanishing

We may be evolving into a world of very few birds. This evolutionary process may have started so slowly that few of us took notice. But now it is happening so quickly that before we know it we won't be able to correct our mistakes. Many tune out the barrage of environmental complaints that are aired so frequently. Some people think that if we don't have a direct connection to nature, there is no need for individual concern. Rain forest destruction, wetlands loss, chemical poisoning, mismanaged forest reserves, oil contamination, urban sprawl, acid rain, ozone depletion, polluted water supplies, rampant refuse, exhausted resources,

170

and pilfered and littered oceans. You can see all these things and get a pretty good idea of where the needs of birds and other natural creatures rank. Through the constant bombardment of updates on natural resource misuse, we continually miss the simple truths of ecology. We cannot seem to separate our needs from our wants.

Silent Invasion

The morning damp and still,
Before the warming sun.
The meadowlark at work,
The owl is almost done.
The sounds that fill the air,
Are those I've heard before.
They seem a bit more quiet now,
A dimming of the roar.
Could it be so slowly,
That the sounds I love are lost?
To a generation farther on,
Who cannot grasp the cost?
Never have upon their ears,
The sounds I hear today.
And never know the loss exists,
Because time steals away.
Perhaps this thief has had me too,
And robbed me of the sound,
My father's father used to hear,
Some generations down.   —DICK E. BIRD

No Bird Is an Island

If you enjoy watching and feeding birds, you realize that no bird is an island, and that there are many things we still do not understand about them (besides sneezing and belching) and the complex niches they fill. The birds at your feeder are an important part of everything around them. They were not just thrown into their present-day niche; it took millions of years, lots of adjustment, and a whole bunch of trial and error. Scientists are now predicting that during the next three decades, as many as three-quarters of the species inhabiting the Earth today could become extinct. As incredible as this is to believe, there is proof of it taking place every day, everywhere — not only in faraway and remote areas of the world but right in your backyard.

"When you said you needed more habitat, they must have thought you meant roads!"

Each bird is fitted to a special habitat where it can find the water, food, and shelter needed for its survival. As this habitat is altered or destroyed, so follow the inhabitants of this space. As time goes on, wild birds will become more and more our most important wildlife. At this time in our history, we are developing millions of acres a year and destroying valuable natural habitat. It is a struggle between self-interest and making the right decisions for future generations.

We tend to make excuses about why we should try to save endangered species. They have secrets we have not been able to gather yet. They also have possible medicinal value, and they can be valuable as sources of scientific data. We must stop looking at birds and other wildlife in an economic sense, a social sense, a poetic sense, and even a scientific sense. Why not think of them as an important part of creation that needs no excuse to exist, no reason to inhabit a given space, no justification to act in a natural role?

Survival of any species depends on sufficient resources and the ability to compete for those resources. Extinction comes from the inability to obtain necessary resources. We as a species have never run out of resources because we have succeeded in taking resources from other species. Our understanding of the world around us becomes more clear only as the effects of our mistakes compound. A life-form with no tangible economic value has little chance to survive in a future of shrinking resources.

Some people have used the word 'linkage' to describe how things interact with one another. It explains a change of events caused by rattling the chain at any point. Linkage is an excellent way to define nature. There is a link between who we are and how we relate to our surroundings.

Your own backyard will tell you more about the condition of the planet than reading the summations from the Earth Summit. Birds face so many problems every day: Pesticides, herbicides, cats, dogs, oil spills, over-development, timber harvest, ground water contamination, industrial waste, obstructed flyways, light pollution, noise pollution, rain forest destruction, poaching, roadkill, powerline collisions, and poisoning.

But your birds' problems will become your problems.

Recap and Reinforce

• Besides The Rand McNally Atlas, birds use navigational tools, such as an inner magnetic field, instinct, heavenly configurations, food sources, landmarks, and imprinted directions.

• Birds are known to be ten to twenty times more sensitive than mammals to commonly used pesticides.

• 50,000 synthetic chemicals have been developed since World War II — 12,000 have shown up in our drinking water so far.

• The periodic shedding of feathers is called molting.

• Some birds migrate at night because it's easier to travel when the kids are asleep.

• Birds are considered our most accessible wildlife.

• Birds do not flap their wings. Bird wings are stationary, the body moves up and down.

• Scientists believe the cardinal is one bird that has extended its range because of birdfeeding.

• Birds fluff their feathers in the winter to create natural insulation. They also shiver, which helps produce additional body heat.

Dear Dick E. Bird

Dear Dick E. Bird:

My parents have been putting me through college and paying for everything. I will graduate with honors this spring and they are very proud. I am going to be an ornithologist. When I was a freshman, I told my parents and they thought it was a foot doctor. It made them so proud that I was going to be a doctor. I didn't have the heart to tell them I was going to study birds, so I just went along with it. How can I break the news to them before graduation? They are already lining up friends with foot problems for my new practice.

—Real Heel in Mobile

Dear Heel:

You are going to need a foot doctor just to get yours out of your mouth, and then you are still going to have to worry about your dad's. About the only advice I can give you is to plead temporary insanity. Tell them you thought it was foot doctoring too! Look shocked when you get your diploma and it says ornithology is the study of birds. Or combine the two and specialize in pigeon toes.

—Keep Smilin', Dick E. Bird

Dear Dick E. Bird

I have a goldfinch that will sit right on the perch while I fill the feeder. He looks scared to death, but he won't move. He just kind of looks up at me in sheer terror. Do you think there is something wrong with him? My husband says he is probably one seed short of a full load.   —Wondering in Wilmington

175

Dear Wonder Woman:

I think this little fellow is probably one seed over a full load. He sat there and took on too much cargo for liftoff. He could be just a overly friendly customer or maybe real greedy. In any event, whether he trusts you or not, enjoy his company and your opportunity to see him up close.　　　　— Keep Smilin', Dick E. Bird

Tongue-in-Beak Tidbits

Test your knowledge and understanding of man's connection to birds.

APPLY FEATHERED FACTS

1. Why are we like tacks on environmental issues?
2. What is often referred to as the most important barometer of the environment?
3. What familiar sounds can you hear in Beethoven's *Sixth Symphony*?

DISCUSSION TOPICS

1. Besides providing food and an alarm system, why did ancient Greeks raise geese?
2. What is the oldest known field guide to birds?
3. What did early man most admire in birds?
4. What bird did Audubon say would never become extinct?

BIRD-BRAINED TRIVIA

1. The flesh of small birds was one of the original ingredients in what pie?

2. What are the two possible chances of finding ivory-billed wood peckers still surviving in the wild?

3. What do miners use for gas and environmentalists use as examples?

4. How did the ancient Greeks communicate the results of the first Olympic games prior to ESPN?

5. What instructions did Noah give the robins on his Ark?

6. How did Scandinavian parents tell their children where babies come from?

7. What bird did Ringo, John, Paul, and George say would sing in the dead of night?

8. If you use the original recipe, how many blackbirds would you bake in a pie?

AND THE ANSWER IS—

Apply Feathered Facts: 1. Because we are pointed in one direction and headed in another. 2. Bird populations. 3. Bird calls. **Discussion Topics:** 1. To provide feathers for their arrows. 2. As many as one hundred centuries ago, folks were painting birds on cave walls and taking note of their habits. 3. Flight. 4. Passenger pigeon. **Bird-Brained Trivia:** 1. Mincemeat. 2. Slim and none. 3. Canaries. 4. Homing pigeons. 5. Go easy on the worms; I only brought two. 6. They simply told the children the stork brought them. 7. Blackbird. 8. Four and twenty (twenty-four).

The depth of winter is fathomed in the sounds of birds, carried through the fields on musical sheets of wind. —DICK E. BIRD

7•

Recipes, Home Brews, Methods, and Wing Tips

Why Gamble?

There are a number of ingredients I refer to as the "Why gamble?" group. Red dye, peanut butter, and spicy seed are at the top of that list. The short answer to all the suspicion of whether these usages are harmful to birds is "Why gamble?"

There is absolutely no need to add red food coloring to hummingbird sugar/water mixtures. The argument is whether red dye causes kidney and liver damage in birds and the possibilities of egg softening. It certainly won't do any harm if not used.

The question of birds possibly choking on peanut butter has been around for years, and I have had people tell me conclusively that it does and does not happen. There are many recipes around to resolve this issue. One original recipe was born out of the concern that peanut butter alone might be too sticky and choke some birds. Why gamble? Mix one part peanut butter and one part lard. Mix one part flour and one part cornmeal. Then mix the two parts together and you have a marvelous meal your birds will love to not choke on.

179

Will seed mixed with natural cayenne pepper additives thwart squirrels? More importantly, will it be harmful to birds? Why gamble?

Bind Your Birdseed

A unique way to present assorted seeds and nuts to your birds and squirrels is to mold them into a form and place it into a suet holder or on a nail in the yard. In order to do this, you need a binding agent such as suet or egg whites. A very simple recipe for this is three egg whites whipped until stiff and then several cups of seed or nuts folded in. Using a cup, or some other container, mold the seed mixture into a form and place it on a greased pan and bake at 300°F for thirty minutes or until it

"I choked on your stupid peanut butter, Ernie. You'll be hearing from my lawyer!"

hardens. You might as well throw the eggshells into this recipe also. Birds always like their grit. It helps their digestion.

With this recipe, you can control costs on block seed mixes, select the mix you prefer, and do a lot more baking with recipes that call for egg yolks. You can also feed the yolks to your dog. It will give him a beautiful coat and high cholesterol.

You can add dried fruit and even some veggies. Who knows, maybe birds will eat their carrots!

You don't need seventeen recipes to feed your birds. Suet mixes can be altered to include crushed dog biscuits, seed mixes, granola, vegetables, coconut, graham crackers, fruit, popcorn, and any number of food items your birds enjoy. Don't forget nuts, which are popular with all kinds of birds. The nut's storehouse of fat and protein makes it a great choice for a menu additive to your backyard smorgasbord. You might also want to experiment with setting out cheese, raw coconut, cornbread, watermelon pulp, and vegetable seeds. There are different strokes for different folks, and I have heard the same for birds.

True Zit

My wife she made some candy,
And, boy, did it smell good.
She mixed it with the sweetest sweets,
And all the nuts she could.

She used the finest caramel,
Coconut, and fudge.
And cooled it on the patio,
I could hardly wait to judge.

But when we went to check it,
All we found were crumbs and bits.
And soon we found the culprits,
All our squirrelly friends had zits.   —DICK E. BIRD

Suet

Nothing gives a home that birdfeeding feeling like the smell of beef kidney suet on the stove. You can get zits just from smelling the stuff. Suet is raw beef fat found around the loins and kidneys—and in backyards all over the world. It is the best food choice for attracting woodpeckers. If you want to render your own suet instead of buying commercially manufactured blocks, ask your butcher if he will grind it up for you. This will save a lot of work at home.

Melt your ground suet down in a double boiler and save the liquid suet in a cooling container. Remelting this cooled liquid will produce a very hard suet mix when it cools a second time. This makes it last much longer outside. This second cooling period is when you want to introduce your recipe additives. Be sure you allow it to begin cooling and thickening before combining additives. Otherwise, they will float to the top.

Some birds prefer a softer single-melt suet that won't bother their dentures. Offer them a little of both.

Suet mixes are an easy-access, high-energy food source, especially for calorie-counting winter birds who are looking for more, not less.

My Birds Are Vegetarians

If you prefer not to have your birds sup on suet, you can still offer them fat and protein using ingredients that mix into a nonsuet subsistence. In a large bowl mix two cups of crunchy peanut butter, one cup cornmeal, one cup oatmeal, and a cup and a half of assorted fruit, nuts, seed, and dried eggshells. Blend it thoroughly and don't shake hands with anyone. Form this material into any shape that makes you feel good and freeze it. Making small portions will allow you to dole it out as it is needed.

"If it's so easy, you go find nuts!"

Another nonsuet version that appeals to many birds is equal parts peanut butter, vegetable shortening, flour, and cracked corn, and to this whole mess add three or four parts cornmeal. Freeze it in small portions and dole it out to your drooling birds.

Too Many Cooks Spoil the Suet

Suet is like a casserole: You can mix it a thousand and one different ways. There are many wonderful suet recipes and commercial suet products available that your birds will appreciate. You can make all your birds happier than a crow in corn with simple mixes or detailed delicacies. Commercial suet blocks are usually pure kidney beef suet rendered to a hardened state that lasts much longer than the raw suet you would find at the meat counter.

At one time butchers had cold hands but warm hearts, and they used to give away their suet. But that has all changed as birdfeeding has become a billion-dollar industry. Now suet is priced per pound. Because of the demand for feeding birds, meat departments now often wrap suet in corded material, ready for hanging. If you are the adventuresome type, you will not use this dull high-tech hanging suet. It could possibly bore your birds. If you really want to mess up the kitchen, try this.

Grind up a few pounds of suet and melt it in a double boiler. Let it cool and harden.

Once you have remelted the suet, measure out six liquid cups and as it is cooling, mix in three cups of crunchy peanut butter, three cups of cornmeal, and ten mixed cups of seed, raisins, chopped nuts, cracked and whole corn, eggshells, dried berries, and cereal. Use your imagination. You do not have to be a French chef to make suet treats for birds. You only need a flair for fat. (That's why most French chefs make good birdfeeders.)

If your spouse has been saying, "I would like to see you in the kitchen more often," I can guarantee after you make this recipe your spouse will never want to see you again—in the kitchen or otherwise.

Nectar Notations

People have many questions about what to offer hummingbirds. The issues have been studied extensively and, without going into all the debate, here are a few things you definitely *do not* want to do.

Do not offer hummingbirds honey.

Do not use red food coloring to emphasize your sugar water offering.

Do not put too much sugar in your mixture.

Do not let mixture ferment in hot weather. Replace it often.

The correct sugar/water mixture is four to one: four cups of water to one cup of sugar because it is very close to the makeup of flower nectar (sucrose and water). You can boil it for a good mix and to help retard fermentation, but you do not have to. It dissolves quickly and does not lose any nutrients because there are none to begin with. Do not increase the amount of sugar to this solution because it will cause digestive problems for the birds.

Delicious Dough

Mix two cups of water and one cup of sugar. Grind and double-melt one cup of suet over low heat in a large container. As the suet begins to cool, mix in the sugar /water mixture along with two cups of yellow cornmeal. This mixture will form a soft dough. Gradually stir in two cups of all-purpose flour to stiffen the dough. This makes a good consistency for use on pinecones or in holes drilled in dead branches.

Let Them Eat Cake

This is a real crummy idea. In a large bowl, mix two cups of flour, half a teaspoon of baking powder, and one teaspoon of baking soda. In a separate pan boil one cup of water, one cup of sugar, one cup of raisins, and half a cup of lard for ten minutes. Mix in the dry ingredients along with a few nuts. Pour the whole mixture into a greased cake pan. Bake it for twenty-five minutes at 325°F, and you are ready for a bird-day party. You can spread some of this mix on the ground for those who have never developed table manners.

Another cake recipe that birds love takes little time and effort. Melt two cups of peanut butter and two cups of lard in a large pan. Once melted, add four cups of cornmeal, one cup of flour, a quarter cup of sugar, and four cups of quick-cook oats. Mix this well and let it cool in whatever forms you choose.

Taking a Powder

If you are having problems with cats and dogs showing up at the feeder and disrupting your birds, you might want to try this recipe for cat- and dog-repellent powder.

Place the following ingredients in a bag and shake together for several minutes. Be careful not to inhale the dust or get it in your eyes. Sprinkle perimeter where desired.

Cayenne pepper	1 ounce
Powdered mustard	1½ ounces
Flour	2½ ounces

Bluebird Banquet

Early spring is often a stressful time for birds that return before the mild weather does. Spring can be elusive. Even the groundhog has his doubts when it actually arrives. Only "the shadow knows." At that time of the year some birds, like the bluebird, will often come more readily to offerings that would not ordinarily attract them when normally desired natural food sources are available. Mealworms are an excellent food source, but you can also use them to bait the birds to come to suet-based mixes.

Mealworm Ranch

Mealworms make an excellent main course or hors d'oeuvre. This offering is an excellent way to bring in birds that otherwise may not show up for seed. You can buy mealworms at a pet supply store or grow your own. Raising them is a very easy, clean, and odorless operation—a cubic-foot farm is all you need. A small garbage can is good, but you can use smaller containers. Mix a couple gallons of bran. You can buy this at a local farm feed supplier. To this add a couple pounds of cornmeal. Slice two apples and two potatoes in half and lay them on top of the mixture face-down. Cover all of this with burlap or a couple of dish towels.

The most important part of ranching is starting with good stock. You can buy yourself a few dozen head of mealworms at most any pet supply store. Corral them in your bran can, cover them, and store in a cool area. You do not have to water them; just replace the apples and potatoes once a week.

> *A bug in a bird is worth two bugs in a bush.*

The next question is: "What came first, the beetle or the egg?" In this case, it was the worms—remember? The worms will grow to about an inch. They will turn into pupas and then into black beetles. The beetles lay eggs and the eggs turn into more worms. You harvest some of the worms and they turn into birdfeed by placing them in a shallow plastic container. These little critters cannot climb up the side of your birdfeeder corral, so you can run your ranch topless at the feeding stage.

Baking Your Birdseed

Some people actually bake their birdseed to prevent it from germinating. It seems like a crazy idea, since birds are coming to the feeder preloaded with non-baked, prefertilized, ready-to-plant seed from the neighbor's feeder, and will subconsciously deposit it whenever the spirit moves them. Thistle seed is commercially sterilized because it is an imported non-native weed seed. If you do plan a practice of birdseed baking, I would suggest a large commercial oven you could also use as a clothes dryer. Ten minutes at 300°F should kill the will of any seed with a need to breed.

Bird-Friendly Weed Wasters

This formula will work for spot-treating weeds. Mix one tablespoon liquid soap in half a gallon of food-grade vinegar. Use in a spray bottle with a nozzle that can be adjusted to a fine stream. Apply this mixture during a very hot part of the day.

Urine for a Surprise

There are concoctions available that will supposedly scare problem critters from the garden plot or birdfeeder. Most of them include predator urine. Garden centers and feed stores often carry these products. Trying to get a fox to cooperate is almost impossible. There are products available in a wafer form that is red fox urine-impregnated. This scent is supposed to make the average squirrel haul tail for the tall timber. If your squirrels are not urine connoisseurs, you might want to try other varieties around your birdfeeder. Just don't let the neighbors catch you.

Recap and Reinforce

• White vinegar is considered a poor sterilizing agent, but it is sold in a spray bottle containing a higher concentration of acetic acid than contained in table vinegar.. This household cleaning product will also work to clean birdbaths and birdfeeding apparatus.

• Ten minutes of contact time by a household bleach solution of one tablespoon per gallon of water is all that is needed to kill birdbath algae. Rinse thoroughly.

• Frozen suet is easier to handle and ease out of containers. Put it out in small portions to prevent spoilage. Keep it out of direct sunlight and a squirrel's right-of-way. A suet cage will help keep your furball from becoming a grease monkey.

• Buy seed at least fifty pounds at a time for the best economy. Mark Twain would advise putting all your seed in one can and watching that can. I advise buying in quantity and putting it in several metal containers in a cool dry area with a Pinkerton guard.

• Summer suet feeding will not turn birds into greaseballs, and neither will it cause matted feathers. Birds are messy eaters, but not that messy.

Dear Dick E. Bird

Dear Dick E. Bird

I fill the feeders more than my husband. I mix all the humming-bird nectar. I render all the suet and clean all the feeders most of the time. Does that make me the feeder filler or the fool?

—Faithful in Philadelphia

Dear Faith:

That makes you the fulfilled filler and your husband the fatigued fool, perhaps with the emphasis on "fat." The ornithological term for a nonfilling feeder foreman is "torpor." He tries to hide his laziness with a facade of managerial skills, but the plain truth is that he just doesn't want to get up out of his La-Z-Boy® and leave the boob tube. I don't mean to be too hard on your husband, but if he hasn't been out of his chair lately, you might want to check him for a pulse.

—Keep Smilin', Dick E. Bird

Dear Dick E. Bird:

I have two questions about my hummers. Will a cold nectar mixture on frosty mornings cause them to suffer from hypothermia and will they hitch rides on geese during migration?

— Puzzled in Paducah

Dear Puzzled:

Some researchers contend that hummingbird feeders with perches allow the birds to sit stationary, especially on cool mornings, and take on enough cold sugar water to cause a slight hypothermic condition. Some feel if they were forced to hover naturally, this would not occur. The ride-sharing rumor has been around for a long time. It makes no biological sense that they would. Geese and hummers are not on the same time schedule or route. It would make sense to conserve on energy and hitch a ride here and there when it was convenient. I have read unconfirmed reports by hunters who said they found hummers in the down of downed geese, but none of those reporting were given blood alcohol tests. I have also read historical material with reference to Native Americans finding hummers in cranes they were able to trap. NASA has proven its possibility by shipping the shuttle piggyback-and-forth many times. You have to remember, it wasn't that long ago that bird experts said migrants went to the moon for the winter. Hopefully, we will continue healthy wildlife populations so that we can someday answer all the questions we have.

— Keep Smilin', Dick E. Bird

Tongue-in-Beak Tidbits

The recipe for success is to comprehend your intake and pretend to understand your output. This book will not make you an ornithologist, but if you do these chapter studies, everyone will think you are. Only you will know your true avian deficiency level.

APPLY FEATHERED FACTS

1. What would be a natural suet source for birds?
2. Should kitchen grease from bacon be used to mix with birdfeeding recipes?
3. How many pecks does it take for a bird to eat a bushel of seed?
4. What do some people feel will help their arthritis and clean the birdbath?

DISCUSSION TOPICS

1. What happens when you add dog food to bird mix recipes?
2. Why should you melt suet twice?
3. Should you ever feed honey to hummingbirds?
4. What is a cheap way to display suet?

BIRD-BRAINED TRIVIA

1. Is red the only color hummingbirds are attracted to?
2. What three birds could also be kitchen utensils?
3. What happens when geese eat too much sweet corn?
4. What fruits do birds like to eat?
5. How do nuthatches find insects on the sides of trees?
6. Why do birds feed their young fireflies?
7. Do birds share information on food location?
8. What is one of the best recipes for attracting birds to the yard?

AND THE ANSWER IS—

Apply Feathered Facts: 1. Animal carcasses. 2. Yes, but sparingly. Stay away from using products that might contain a lot of seasonings or other additives. 3. Four. 4. Vinegar. **Discussion Topics:** 1. Your birds will begin barking up the wrong tree. 2. Reheating will make it harder and it will not spoil as quickly. 3. Never. 4. Onion bag. **Bird-Brained Trivia:** 1. No, but many people think so because most commercial hummingbird feeders are decorated in red. 2. Dipper, skimmer, and nutcracker. 3. They get goose pimples. 4. Birds will go bananas over fruit at the feeder. Besides bananas, try raisins, currants, sliced apples, oranges, and jelly. 5. Listen to their barks. 6. They want bright kids. 7. It is believed some do. 8. Landscaping with plants that serve as a food source, cover, and nesting site.

8•

Shocking Growth of the Bird Business

The Birdsnest Boarding House Wrental Units

In the spring of 1980 my wife, Gaila, and I were into our third year of working our way around North America. We were headed for Alaska and had just pulled our trailer over 1,200 miles of every kind of dirt road known to man. We stopped in Tok Jct., Alaska, for the night. Across the road stood a food cache, a stilted log cabin structure that trappers would store their supplies in, during the winter, so large and small critters could not reach them. To most people it probably looked like a worn-out miniature fire tower. But to me it looked like the perfect birdhouse design. As the years rolled under our wheels and we continued to travel, work and explore various parts of the country, we fine-tuned our birdhouse to also function as a feeder. If the birds didn't move in, the chimney popped off and it could be filled with seed. They came with a deed and everyone who bought one became an FTB

(For The Birds) Broker. We had brokers in every state and paid a five percent commission on sales. We caused quite a stir and one day the Michigan Attorney General's office called and said they had complaints we were selling houses without a real estate license.

My wife Gaila decided to send Willard Scott of the "Today" show a feeder/house. I told her he wouldn't put it on television because he only did festivals. She had just read his book *The Joy of Living* and said, "I don't care. I like him and I'm going to send him one." We were still living in our Airstream, parked next to a small cottage we rented and turned into a birdfeeder factory. As I nailed away on feeders with the "Today" show on in the background, I thought I heard the word "birdfeeder." Bryant Gumbel and Willard Scott had our birdfeeder with the chimney off, and they were trying to stick a Georgia peach in the seed opening. They fooled with it for several minutes before Willard said, "This is the best birdfeeder ever built." And Bryant said, "It's from Dick and Gaila Mallery, Acme, Michigan."

That's when the phone blew off the wall. As the show went West, I kept raising the price. We had a price increase for every time zone the "Today" show moved into. Over the past twenty-five years we have built thousands of Birdsnest Boarding Houses and sold them all over North America without using distributors. The design was cloned by crafters and manufacturers from Maine to California but no one had the fun we did in marketing this unique feeder/house that offered One Low Payment, No Interest, No Closing Costs, and Immediate Occupancy. It will Not Increase Taxes, Enhances Your Property, Meets All Local Zoning Requirements, No Title Insurance Necessary, No Building Permit

Required, No Points, No Inspectors To Hassle With, No Sub-contractors To Chase After, No Survey Costs, No Utilities, Little Site Preparation, and All Pre-Engineered.

The Story

The birdfeeding industry has hundreds of stories on how people turned an outside interest into an inside and very profitable business. As consumers turned birdfeeding into an industry that generates billions in sales annually, every company that made a wood, metal or plastic product began designing and marketing products that could tap into these dollars. One example is a company that made electric bug zappers. They replaced their zapper with a seed dispenser, which is probably a much better bug-control device since birds target agricultural insect pests and bug zappers randomly destroy anything that happens by.

This swell of interest has been good for the growth of the birdfeeding industry but not always beneficial for the consumer or the birds. In many products function does not fit design, and in some cases function was not even considered in design. It is very important that consumers have some knowledge of wildlife needs. Before making product-buying decisions they should know what is required to make attracting wildlife successful. Two of the most important would have to be visibility and cleanability.

The expanded retail market in specialty wild bird products has improved choice, quality and availability. This is especially true in the seed market. Prior to this revolution, birds were eating more and enjoying it less. Eating out all the time can lead to many problems if you are not careful what you eat. Birds eat out all the time. It is our job as responsible backyard bird feeders to make meals complete, healthy, and enjoyable. We are not only bird feeders, we are avian nutritionists. Birds do not like diets. If you put your birds on a diet, they will disappear. Birds need to eat constantly. They are always refueling and preparing for takeoff. Birds lead a very intense life-style and digest food so rapidly that, in some cases, it can actually end up on your windshield 20 minutes after intake.

Think About Your Birds When You Buy

When you make a buying decision, on birdfeeders and nesting boxes, consider function as well as design. With feeders, think about visibility. Birds being able to see the seed offering is your best advertising. Seed capacity is important, as well as adequate perching area for the species you hope to attract. Bigger is not always better. Frequent filling will help keep your offerings clean and fresh.

How a feeder fills is very important. If you need three hands to fill a feeder that is awkward to open, you will turn your desire to feed birds into a chore. Look for good sturdy materials and solid craftsmanship. Solid construction is important, especially if you live near a squirrel. Another important consideration is a weather-proof design. A seed dispenser that sheds moisture will help prevent feed contamination. In warm weather, mold will invade wet bird feed.

Seed dispensers, birdbaths, nectar jars, suet holders and even squirrel feeders, should be cleaned on a regular basis. Do not make this practice more of a job than it already is. Buy products from manufacturers that have already taken cleaning ease into consideration.

Equipment:
• Birdbath heaters are controlled thermostatically and hydrostatically. The power is automatically cut when temperature is reached or if water completely evaporates.

• The best-constructed squirrel-proof feeders should be steel. Pay attention to the metal coating so you won't have to deal with rust immediately. Plastic will have more of a chance of falling victim to a chewsy squirrel.

• Plastic birdfeeders constructed of tough polycarbonate material will be the best defense against raiding rodents.

• Wire squirrel-resistant tube feeders can be very effective against squirrels with a short reach.
• A vertical-perch thistle tube feeder will help discourage house finches and allow goldfinches immediate available seating. A commercial seed sock will allow open access to every bird on the block.

• Squirrel-a-Whirl can keep furballs busy. Every five minutes a squirrel isn't eating seed, you save twenty dollars.

• Nectar-feeder-buying-decision questions should include capacity (bigger is not always better), filling convenience, number of outlets, perching, opening size, bee guards and mounting options.

Historical and Hysterical Birdfeeder Facts

Most people do not spend a lot of time thinking about the world history of birdfeeding, but its origins are at least as important as who might be buried in Grant's tomb.

We do know that Native Americans hung out gourds to attract nesting birds. It was most likely for insect control, because I am sure they did not have a clue that attracting birds was going to become so popular. I have always felt that the first field guides were written by early poets and nature writers,

Dodson Wren House

expressing thoughts of their surroundings. Actual field guides were printed prior to 1900 but were very narrow in scope. The earliest field guide in my collection is material authored by Chester Reed and published by Doubleday, Page & Company. It is copyrighted 1906 and already warning of the destruction of habitat and loss of bird life.

> **Birds are theirs that enjoy them.**

The first line in the introduction reads, "It is an undisputed fact that a great many of our birds are becoming more scarce each year, while a few are, even now, on the verge of extinction."

The first species covered in the guide is a color drawing of the "Carolina paoquet." Now extinct, this guide lists the bird's range as "Formerly the southern states, but now confined to the interior of Florida, and, possibly, Indian Territory."

Many people, having just discovered the joys of feeding and viewing wild birds, have the misconception that birdfeeding is a yuppie interest that started yesterday. In reality, modern-day birdfeeding has been seriously evolving for over a hundred years.

Joseph H. Dodson of Kankakee, Illinois, had an early love for birds. He said they made his life happier and that he wanted to spread the inspiring influence of birds to others. He claimed, in the early 1920s, "There is a great difference between my houses, and the commercial bird houses that are built only to sell. My houses are designed after forty years of loving studies of birds and their habits..." This guy was promoting year-round birdfeeding and landscaping to attract birds, and preaching the importance of cleaning feeders and houses in 1912. He was also warning people about the devastating number of birds killed by cats annually. His early catalog shows deluxe martin houses that look more like intricate Southern mansions. His product line included birdhouses, birdbaths, birdfeeders, and sparrow traps. For those of you who are still trying to outfox your fox squirrel, consider that Dodson was working on outsmarting them 75+ years ago. He invented squirrel baffles that would actually grow. In his catalog he states, "For years I have given this subject thought, my idea's being to bring out a device that would not only keep the cat, squirrel and other animals out of the trees where your birds are nesting, but would expand with the growth of the tree." Dobson would ship his baffle in any length to fit the circumference of any tree. He also sold suet cakes for fifty cents a pound.

The explosive growth in the birdfeeding industry we see today began just prior to World War II as several manufacturers saw a possible niche in the gardening market and began building an interest in attracting birds to feeders and nesting boxes. America was on the sprawl. The country was on the move to the city in the form of suburbia, leisure was infiltrating lifestyle, and landscaping was the solution for satisfying a yearning of a countryside remembered.

Hyde Bird Feeder Company

In 1938, Donald B. Hyde, Sr., designed and made a unique wild bird feeder for his wife, Joyce. It could be fastened onto a windowsill with screws and could be filled from inside the house. Birds quickly learned to visit it, and she could watch them feed right outside her window. It wasn't long before their neighbors and friends wanted feeders just like it. This model, and others like it, soon became the basis for a part-time business in addition to Don Hyde's wholesale lumber business. The original windowsill model was part of the Hyde line for fifty years.

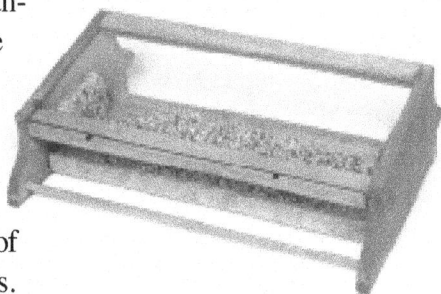

Following some serious research into nesting habits of wild birds, Don also began designing and building birdhouses. By 1943, he moved the wood shop to his lumber yard in Waltham, Mass., to provide more space for his growing business. The Florence Calkins Lab, manufacturing suet cakes combined with seeds or peanut hearts, also moved in. Hyde bought every suet product they could make to sell to local garden shops along with his feeders and houses.

During World War II, there was a severe shortage of lumber for uses other than the war effort. Hyde located a large supply of scrap mahogany at a PT boat yard on the Gulf of Mexico and had it shipped to Waltham. Mahogany birdfeeders and houses kept the little business going in the absence of the regular supply of white pine.

The business grew slowly but steadily, after the war, as Don travelled the eastern half of the country selling an increasing number of models. However, in 1953 he died suddenly. His son, Don, Jr., was learning the lumber business at a sawmill in Arkansas after graduating from college. He returned to Waltham and joined his mother, running the lumber business and the bird products business.

The Korean War had again reduced the supply of lumber for the wholesale business. It was decided to phase out of the lumber and concentrate on birdhouses and feeders. Growth continued slowly but steadily during the next twenty years. In 1968, Don purchased the Ardsley Woodcraft Products Co., a manufacturer of redwood planters, window boxes and bird feeders. A new 12,000 sq. ft. addition was built at the old lumber yard to accommodate the increased production.

From the 1940s through the 1990s, the Hyde Bird Feeder Company was a leader in introducing new wild bird products. Test sites around the country were used to ensure bird-friendly design and anti-squirrel effectiveness of potential new products.

Over this period, some two dozen patents were issued, both to Don Sr. and Don Jr., covering a wide range of innovative and successful products and designs for feeders.

Duncraft

Gil Dunn was a World War II veteran, and a Manhattan native, who loved the out of doors (he was an avid fisherman and canoeist). Newly settled in New Hampshire in the late 1940s, he invented a windowsill birdfeeder and decided to go into business for himself. His birdfeeder was unique. Made of masonite, it clipped on a wooden windowsill, had seed wells, a cup for water, and a rotating "waiting station" made of wooden doweling. He called it the Flight Deck, because birds' alighting on it reminded him of planes he had seen landing on aircraft carrier decks in the Pacific. He made each Flight Deck by hand. It was immediately popular and sold through the mail via advertising in newspapers and magazines. Dunn went on to patent this feeder as well as several others. Dunn used his home and yard for field testing. There were always ten or so feeders in use — on the windowsills and hanging in the beech trees. A one-man business, he manufactured feeders, houses and baths, and he created the Duncraft catalog — the first national mail order catalog of feeders, bird foods, baths, accessories and bird-motif gifts.

Droll Yankees

The birdfeeding industry's short history experienced its first Renaissance around 1969 when Peter Kilham of Barrington, Rhode

Island, decided to replace a squirrel-damaged wooden birdfeeder. Peter's approach to the birdfeeding industry was not one of business. In fact, he hated business. His approach was, obviously, engineering, a love for nature and fine art. The replacement feeder he built from scrap pieces of clear plastic tubing and various metal parts he had lying around his machine shop created an industry within an industry. A large percentage of feeders on the market today are still based on his original tube-feeder designs. His knowledge of birds and their needs enabled him to "build the better mousetrap," or birdfeeder, in this case. He considered the distance from a songbird's feet to its beak when planning seed openings and, most importantly, a simple cleaning design.

What Peter Kilham finally designed seems to be the perfect solution for dispensing seed to birds. It is eye appealing, allows you and your birds to view the seed supply, adequately protects the seed from moisture, controls seed flow, helps discourage larger birds you may not want on your guest list, and is a modern design constructed of space-age materials and innovative technology. Kilham seems to have thought of everything when he created this product for this purpose. He blended into his design the ease of filling, durability, mounting options, and convenience for both bird and bird feeder (that's you).

I can remember seeing Peter's first commercial tube feeder hanging in a garden center. I was amazed. Many people were and sales exploded. One of his first orders went to Bloomingdales. The retailer hung his feeders all over their New York store and ordered 800 more. A few days later, Bloomingdale's called to ask where the feeders were. Peter told them they had been sent. After checking, Bloomingdale's called back and said the whole 800 had been sold before they had time to put them in inventory.

Peter's original Droll Yankees business, started in 1960, had been making phonograph records of old New England stories. They were a specialty item that did not make him a living, so he bought out his partners and began recording bird songs and natural sounds records. This was more successful and something he always loved to do, but it was still not very profitable. Then came his world-famous tube feeder that changed the way we all look at birds.

The name Droll Yankees comes from Peter's desire to find a "Humorous, sharp and witty" word to use along with Yankee in his recording company's name. In Balzac's Droll Stories he found that word, and now the two will go down in birdfeeding history.

Wild Bird Specialty Stores

The next major event in the development of the birdfeeding industry was the consumer-driven specialty retail market. This gave birdfeeding its own identity. It brought birdfeeding products, from being an "also-ran" item, to prominent shelf space, and specialty stores dedicated to improved product, reliable information, quality seed and more variety in feeding choices.

Several franchises specializing in birdfeeding products gave birth to this market niche in the 1980's. This growth in franchising hundreds of wild bird specialty stores, in the U.S. and Canada, drove explosive growth in sales and interest in birdfeeding and wildlife watching. This success spawned thousands of individual backyard bird feeding and nature stores, birdfeeding-product manufacturing and specialty seed operations.

From this new wave of interest came information sharing and consumer education. The new consumer awareness forced many manufacturers to improve their products. Soon the cute little perches on the front of birdhouses began to disappear, nesting box dimensions became more realistic, and innovation was spurred by the market's momentum.

The Feed Store

I looked behind the counter and all across the store,
I couldn't find a soul around, so I turned and shut the door.
I wanted just a bag of seed, and a suet block or two,
So I headed for the birdie aisle, a place so well I knew.
When I arrived, to my surprise, not a single seed was there,
In fact, the aisle was empty, and all the shelves were bare.
"How could this be?" I asked myself. It's fall, I need this stuff!
When my birds do not get fed , they get a little rough.
With panic in my voice I yelled, to not a faint reply,
How could this be that no one cares, that I am here to buy.
I headed back toward the door, and there my eyes did read,
A sign as big as Texas, explaining 'bout the seed.
I took my time to study it, and find out what it said,
I'm still not sure if it is true, but this is what I read:
Come on in I'm glad you're here, but you will find I'm not.
Help yourself to what you need, though I haven't got a lot.
Ring it up and make your change, there's money in the till,
Or leave a note of what ya took, and I will send a bill.
There's coffee on the old woodstove, and cider in the pan.
Go ahead and sit a spell, but spit into the can.
Mornin' paper's on the counter, go ahead and read.
I'll be back by dinner time, I had to go for seed.

—Dick E. Bird

205

Squirrel-Proof

One of the first attempts at a squirrel-proof feeder hit the market as a weight-activated perching device that shut down the feed opening with the weight of one fat squirrel or several beefy birds. Some of the larger birds and squirrels didn't take long to figure out it only took a little teamwork to out-engineer this new design method. The only problem was, squirrels would fight over who would sit on the weight first and who would eat first.

Squirrelly engineers in the industry then took the design one step further and fine-tuned it to a spring-adjustable weight activation. The perch weight was set by adjusting springs underneath the feeder. This worked much better except a squirrel could hang from the back of the feeder

"When he hits the ground, you run up his pant leg and I'll grab the seed."

by its rear feet toenails, stretch its elastic body all the way across the top of the feeder, and hang off the front upside-down and fill its face with seed. Companies began activating the roof so that fat squirrel's, hanging ten, would close the perch when climbing up top. This only lead to squirrels learning to ride sidesaddle.

This is brilliant engineering, but brilliance does not compete with even the lowest IQ-equipped furball. Another problem with this squirrel-proof technology is the squirrel's ability to leap tall buildings in a single bound. Many times squirrels are able to jump directly into the feeder without ever touching the weight-activated perch. Now they are inside where it is high and dry, sitting on a week's worth of groceries, happier than a cat in a sandbox, and no one can see them.

Squirrel Market

Another major impact on the birdfeeding industry took place when manufacturers finally figured out that a squirrel-feeding market was much stronger than the anti-squirrel market. Both survive today, but the dollars spent on accessories to feed and help squirrels entertain us, far outweigh those spent on so-called squirrel-proof accessories. It is very confusing for squirrels. They have no idea if they are coming or going to dinner, but have no fear, they always appear.

Hot Tongue, Cold Shoulder

I only asked for fifty pounds,
Of bird mix in a bag.
And now I've bought a feeder too,
Me wife, she's gonna nag.
And then before I hit the door,
The feed man says, "Look here."
And now I got a birdbath heater,
Me wife, she's gonna sneer.
I almost make it to me truck,
When I hear the cashier yell,
"One minute, sir. Our special's on,
You need a birdseed bell."
So me, I goes back in again,
And gets a bell of seed.
I know when I get home with these,
Me wife, she will be teed.
But since I'm in such awful straights,
I might just get 'er all.
So I buy enough sunflower,
To last me through the fall.
Me wife's a lovely woman,
And I don't like getting her sore.
So I hide what I can, hang out what I must,
Then throw me hat in the door.
If it don't come back, I'm pretty safe,
And I ease in real light.
But if she's mad then be it so,
Me birds are worth a fight.

—Dick E. Bird

Recap and Reinforce:

• When making a feeder-buying decision, think about: which birds will use it; is it easy to clean; will it keep the seed dry; what is the seating capacity; how much cargo space; is it rugged enough to withstand a rodent attack.

• To discourage bird species, you would rather not have at your feed stations, try specialty feeders that baffle birds of various sizes and abilities. Removing perches can also help discourage some larger birds.

• Before the wild bird industry had a niche of its own, wild bird-feeding supplies were distributed mostly through the pet trades.

• Someone started a rumor that purple martins can eat 2,000 mosquitoes a day. That may be true, but I haven't been able to find anyone who has ever followed a martin around for a day with a counter. Actually, their favorite meal is a dragonfly al a carte, insects which prey on mosquito larvae.

• A thermally controlled dog dish can be used as a heated birdbath. It draws 20 watts and at least that many birds.

• It is an old Scandinavian tradition to set out a small sheaf of unthreshed wheat for birds at Christmas.

• When buying or building birdfeeders, be sure there are no sharp edges or points that may injure birds.

Dick E. Bird

Dear Dick E. Bird:

I have never, in my life, seen so many different birdfeeders and houses as I did recently at a friend's wedding. Most newlyweds end up with forty-seven toasters and no bread. This couple received dozens of feeders and houses, birdbaths and heaters and gift certificates for seed. Do you think these are appropriate gifts? I have always bought toasters because they are always on sale somewhere. Should I start giving bird items or is this tacky? If birds are in vogue, I need to know.

— Vague on Vogue in Vicksburg

Dear Vague:

Wild bird items have become the most popular wedding gift of the past decade. Giving the wrong item at the wrong season is tacky. It also shows how little you know about birds and how out of step you are with current gift-buying trends. It is always safe to check local feed stores and see if the couple has registered their wishes. If you do not agree with social trends and still want to give a traditional gift, it is perfectly all right to give a toaster as a wedding gift—just don't put your name on it!

— Keep Smilin', Dick E. Bird

Dear Dick E. Bird:

I have been feeding birds suet for years. Most of the time I just get it from the butcher, but lately I have been buying commercially packaged suet because it has now become more readily available to me in a variety of mixes. Is there any way to keep those blasted squirrels out? They just consumed my new fruit-flavored suet cake in about ten minutes.

—Greased and Fleeced in Florence

Dear Greased:

Without building a real eyesore, it is hard to fool all the squirrels all the time. My suggestion would be a hanging suet feeder that only allows the suet to be accessed from the bottom. Add to this a solid hanging baffle your squirrel cannot see through. Place it so the little grease ball can't leap to it and then say a quiet little prayer.

You will find that squirrels can conquer this setup, but they will work very hard for what little reward they are able to weasel out of you if you keep your ladder locked in the garage so they can't reach your larder. —Keep Smilin', Dick E. Bird

This is a very important chapter unless you have more money than you do bird brains. Your birds rely on you to supply seed and to stay on the leading edge of birdfeeding technology. Choosing a birdfeeder or house is the most important buying decision you will ever make. Do your homework and success will wing its way into your life and perch forever.

APPLY FEATHERED FACTS

1. Will a heated birdbath greatly increase my electric bill?
2. What was the first contemplated birth control?
3. What two fishing equipment items kill the most birds?
4. What is another name for a birdbath?
5. What is a field guide?

DISCUSSION TOPICS

1. Do you save birds by putting seed out as an offering?
2. What do you call a cement birdfeeder?
3. Is commercially grown thistle seed for birdfeeding produced in North America?
4. What is the ornithological term for a rowdy birdbath?

BIRD-BRAINED TRIVIA

1. What do you call a singular snipe looking into a worm hole?
2. What swallow birdhouse has a confusion of many chambers and multi-stories?
3. What do you call an ornithologist who is also a taxidermist?
4. What can you use to cover-coat wooden nesting boxes to weatherproof them?
5. What can you use to help eliminate window strikes?
6. Can squirrels chew tough cylindrical shaped plastic birdfeeders?
7. Are squirrel baffles effective?
8. What is a good depth for the birdbath?

AND THE ANSWER IS—

Apply Feathered Facts: 1. Very little. 2. Putting a cork in a stork. 3. Lead sinkers and monofilament line. 4. A thirst aid kit. 5. A combined set of instructions that comes with each bird. **Discussion Topics:** 1. Seldom does a seed source save any birds. 2. Hard Rock Cafe. 3. No. Africa and Asia. It is a nonnative weed seed that must be sterilized before entering the U.S. 4. Punch bowl. **Bird-Brained Trivia:** 1. Snoop. 2. A perplexed martin house. 3. A person who knows his stuff. 4. Linseed oil. 5. Anything that will break the reflection or brake the bird. 6. Squirrels can chew anything, especially around the seed outlets on tube feeders. 7. Yes, and so are politicians but not very often. 8. Two inches are recommended.

213

Afterword

Humorist and environmental advocate Dick Mallery, a.k.a. Dick E. Bird, publishes the *The Dick E. Bird News*, a bimonthly newspaper about nature in your backyard and beyond. From his Acme, Michigan headquarters he covers birdfeeding, squirrel self-defense, hiking, travel and humor. *The Dick E. Bird News* includes a tongue-in-beak account of the Best Darned BirdstorieS Ever Told. Mallery says it is the largest underfinanced, overextended "good news" paper in the world.

The 20-page tabloid newspaper covers a wide range of nature-related news from care and feeding of birds, and dealing with squirrelly neighbors, to long-distance hiking and the benefits of caring for the environment. Subscribers to *The Dick E. Bird News* also become HUMMINGBIRDS — Humans Under Misguided Management Involved Nationally Googling Birds In Roosts Dispensing Seeds.

For a sample copy send $1.00 to: P.O. Box 377, Acme, Michigan 49610. Any questions call 1-800-255-5128, E-mail: dickebird@gmail.com, or see a sample on the Internet at: www.thedickebirdnews.com.

"Sitting in the backseat of a 1950 Buick Roadmaster as a kid I heard my father say to my mother, "I should write a book." That thought intrigued me even at the tender age of seven. Forty years later that seed finally sprouted.

Much credit has to go to my family who offer constant encouragement. Especially my parents, who will always be a source of inspiration; my wonderful wife, Gaila, who has supported all of my wild ideas and adventures over the past decades, and our daughter, Maggie, who we call the Vice President of Enthusiasm. Dick E. Bird's *Birdfeeding 101 & Nuts About Squirrels* comes from over 20 years of writing and publishing *The Dick E. Bird News*. Holding this nonadvertising, subscription-driven newspaper together has taken hours of work and constant dedication. Our thousands of subscribers are as much a part of this book as all those involved in putting it together. The grocery bags of mail we receive each month fuel the paper and much of the thought that builds our books.

We are also grateful to Rob Robertson, who listened to our ideas and shared his expertise in designing and constructing a book that would inform and entertain the millions of people that enjoy feeding their birds and building a relationship with their squirrels."

—Richard E. Mallery a.k.a. Dick E. Bird

A Puff of Poppycock

The student asked the scholar,
"What is a Dickie Bird?
It's never in the field guides,
It's never seen or heard!"

The scholar told the student,
"It's a species not so rare.
You can find it very common,
But stop looking in the air."

The student told the scholar,
"I don't think I understand.
You mean it's not a bird of air,
I should look around on land?"

"No, no," said the scholar,
"It's not a bird at all.
It's just a puff of poppycock,
Ajester's rhyming call."

—Keep Smilin', Dick E. Bird

216

The edge of the woods, the splashing tidal pools, and the stream-bordered bog; these are the true intersections of the world.

—DICK E. BIRD

Glossary

M.A. Larkey's Bird Words

Acreage—The age when every bird had at least an acre to himself—before man moved in.

Adaptation—The way in which a bird changes to meet the circumstances in which it finds itself.

Adoption—The way in which a cowbird changes his circumstances to meet his destiny.

Adult—The bird with the grocery bill.

Arboreal—Living in trees.

Backlog—A perching site for birds waiting a turn at the feeder.

Baglag—The elapsed time from the moment you notice the feeder is empty until you actually go to the seed bag and get the refill.

Bigatree—One bird having two mates in the same tree at the same time.

Biodegradable—Capable of being broken down by bacteria into basic elements and compounds.

Birdfeeder—Man's effort to improve his lot.

Birdie—A hole of golf that the player has completed in one stroke less than par. Sometimes golfers get birdies and sometimes birdies get golfers.

217

Birdlesque—The way a bird takes off.

Bleak—A bird that is down in the mouth.

Boring—The Northern coniferous forest, at one time called the boreal before it was clear-cut.

Bottleneck—Position a hummingbird finds himself stuck when trying to get nectar that is good to the last drop.

Buccaneer—The inflated price of corn since the invention of squirrel feeders.

Bushwacker—A sharp-shinned hawk with the ability to snare birds on the wing in the thickest of tangles.

Cache—Ill-gotten grains stashed by squirrels.

Cahoot—An owl partnership.

Casual—A bird that is not supposed to be in your area but never read the book and shows up often.

Cat—A pygmy lion who loves birds, hates dogs, and patronizes human beings.

Catapulp—What you beat your cat into when he gets anywhere near the feeder.

Catwalk—Worn path from the birdfeeder to the bushes.

Caw—A crow's crow.

Cemetery—A place filled with people who thought their birds couldn't get along without them.

Cherk—Clerk at the feed store who refuses to give you any more credit.

Chewitsuet—The condition of soft greasy suet in temperatures below -40°F.

Chiselfiddler—An individual who constantly builds birdfeeders but who is too cheap to fill them.

Civilization—A process of creating more needs than means to supply.

Claustrophobia—Fear of cats getting birds.

Clonetagonistic—A bird picking a fight with its own reflection.

Clutch—A set of eggs laid by one bird in a process called "popping the clutch"; a bird's way of putting the next generation in gear.

Coincide—What you do after you fill the birdfeeder.

Cornbore—A cheapskate who never feeds anything to wild birds except cracked corn.

Courtship—The period during which a female bird decides whether or not she can do any better.

Crackerjack—Currency used to feed birds when the seed money runs out.

Crackerquackers—Southern ducks.

Crepuscular—Active during twilight (dawn and dusk).

Crudbusters—Federal Feeder Fumigators who will confiscate your feeders if you do not clean them once a week.

Cup Nest—Ornithological athletic gear.

Dashboard—Birdfeeder perch most often used for quick exiting.

DDT—Genocide.

Deadline—Discarded fishing line that birds become entangled in.

Debate—De seed dat lures de birds.

Dido—A dead dodo.

Dingleberry—A belled cat in a blueberry bush.

Disastenator—A person who procrastinates so long about fixing the feeder that it finally becomes a disaster.

Divine—De plant where de birds find de berries.

Double-Dipper—Hummingbird drawing nectar from one feeder while eyeballing another.

Doughnate—Placing baked goods out for your birds.

Down—A covering of soft fluffy feathers. Young birds are covered with down before they get up.

Ear-Coverts—The feathers overlying the ears of most birds.
Ecology—Study of the relationship between living things and their environment.

Economy—A puzzling word with a number of definitions. It can mean the large size when buying birdseed and the small size of your wallet after you pay for it.

Ecotist—A person more interested in his environment than himself.

Edible—Good to eat and wholesome to digest, as a worm to a toad, a toad to a snake, a snake to a pig, a pig to a man, and a man to a worm.
Egg—A potential bird; a fowl ball.
Escape Hatch—The act of breaking out of an egg.

Falsie—Plastic owl used to keep starlings out of the garden.
Fasting—Slowing seed intake.
Fauna—The animal life of a region.
Feedback—Fieldmarks found on car windshields.
Feral Cat—A free-ranging roameow with no owner and a flair for feathers.
Fidget—A hungry, impatient fledgling waiting for a meal.
Film—The stuff you are supposed to clean off your birdfeeders once a week.
Flail—Learning to fly.
Flicker—A blinking woodpecker that needs his tracking adjusted.
Flinch—The movement of finches off the birdfeeder when a jay shows up.

Foodgitives—Squirrels known to work more than one neighborhood.

Free-for-all—Ample supplies of seed, suet, and nectar fought over by birds, squirrels, and raccoons in the backyard.

Geronimo—The last word out of a squirrel's mouth when it jumps from a tree to a birdfeeder fifty feet below.

Gibberish—The story a husband gives his wife about being too busy to fill the birdfeeder while holding a fishing pole in both hands.

Gnawty—Squirrels that not only eat all your birdseed but also chew your feeder in half.

Goblin—The way your squirrel was acting before the chase.

Googoology—The study of baby birds.

Gorget—A patch of brightly colored feathers on the chin or throat of some birds.

Gregarious—Living in flocks with a bunch of birds all named Greg.

Gruesome—What happens to the fledglings every time the adult birds make a round-trip from the nest to the food cache.

Guzzle—Ornithological term meaning to digest seed without chewing.

Hari-Kari—Squirrels transporting birdseed from your place to theirs.

Herd—A flock of birds horsing around.

Hoax—Leaving the colored picture, advertising seed, inside your tube feeder so birds will think it is always full.

Honeymoon—The light under which newly mated humming-birds sip nectar.

Hoodoo—Owl pellets.

Hooker—A hawk picking up songbirds at your feeder.

Horde—A herd of birds.

Hozone—Range at which you can hit a squirrel with the garden hose.

Hudder-Mudder—The deep throaty sound made by a spouse when told to fill the feeder when it's -35°F outside.

Huddle—The ornithological term for flocking birds on the fifty-yard line.

Humbug—Fruit fly.

Humdinger—A hummingbird trying to get nectar out of a bluebell.

Hummingbird—An eagle after taxes; a buzzy busybody.

Hummingmummy—A hummingbird that is pressed for time.

Immature—A young bird out on its own but not fully developed in size and color; an adult bird that does not act its age.

Inhale—A squirrel's eating procedure.

Itemize—A hawk's glare while checking out the menu at the birdfeeder.

Ketchup—What the last bird to reach the feeder wants to do.

Knitpicker—Birds that collect yarn put out by humans for the purpose of nest building.

Knocktet—Eight woodpeckers.

Knockturnal—A woodpecker working at night.

Legend—The edge of a nest where many birds get their first flight lesson.

Lichen—A fungi filler used to build hummingbird nests.

Lickety-Spit—A woodpecker tasting spoiled suet.

Liquidate — Breeding season at the birdbath.

Listless — Feeling no inclination toward or interest in marking birds down on paper; a lethargic birdwatcher.

Lore — The space between the eye and the bill.

Minuet — A small amount of suet.

Minuteman — A guy who can make it to the feeder, fill it, and get back to his chair during a sixty-second commercial during a ball game.

Mirage — Imagining a birdbath in the yard.

Miscarry — A male bird bringing nesting material that the female did not order.

Mohawk — A raptor species closely related to Larry and Curly hawks.

Molting — A bird's only downfall.

Monogamous — A one-bird bird.

Mosquito — A small insect designed by God to make us appreciate swallows and bats.

Nectar — The sweet liquid secreted by plants and used by hummingbirds to fuel their turbo-charged engines. Myth has it that nectar is the life-giving drink of the gods.

Niche — The unique way of life of a plant or animal species — where it lives and what it does in the community.

Night Stick — A twig used by a robin to poke around for worms when it wants a midnight snack.

Nitwit — One who feeds sunflower seed in a thistle feeder.

Numbskull — Sensation most birds experience after crashing into picture windows.

Obeseedy — A greedy jay who has let too much seed go to waist.

Oology — The study of eggs.

Oops—The call a blue jay makes when he accidentally or on purpose bumps a nuthatch off the feeder perch.
Ornithology—The scientific study of birds; the branch of zoology that deals with birds.

"We call him Hoover. He can suck seed in without even moving his lips."

Pantry—The tree that holds the birdfeeder.
Park—A pigeon mess hall.
Pasteurize—Where a squirrel walks in front of you with another load of your seed.
Philosopher—To admire a bird as long as it isn't over your head.
Plumage—A bird's entire covering of feathers.
Pokerface—The expression on a squirrel's face as it cleans out your feeder, poking the very last sunflower seed into its mouth.
Pole-Vault—The squirrelly act of jumping twenty feet from a tree limb directly to the feeder, bypassing the pole.
Posthaste—Birds swiftly vacating a fence post when shrieked by a shrike.
Postmark—Indentation on a feeder pole indicating the misjudgment of a jumping squirrel with a splitting headache.
Precocial—Covered with down and able to run around when newly hatched.
Preening—To clean or smooth feathers with the beak.
Prey—Critters captured and consumed by other critters.
Preytell—The way a hawk locates lunch by listening for a songbird bellowing from the beak.
Propagander—Leaning a drunken goose against a wall.
Pterodactyl—The early bird.
Purchase—A cat after a bird.

224

Quicker-Picker-Upper—When a hummingbird tries to get nectar from an outdoor light socket.
Quivershiver—The process of fluffing out down feathers for insulation on cold days.

Raptor—A bird of prey, much like the hawk sitting on your feeder.
Rebound—A bird re-marking his territory after discovering his neighbor is much bigger than he is.
Rectangle—A hawk after crashing into a bush while chasing an elusive songbird.
Redundance—Two-stepping with a whippoorwill.
Relief—The soothing feeling a bird experiences when the trees begin to rebud.
Remark—A bird dropping deposited immediately after you leave the car wash.
Resident—A bird that likes you so much that he stays all year.
Retail—Molting at full price.
Retension—The amount of seed a squirrel can hold while under stress.
Retreat—A bird finding a cache of seed he thought he'd already eaten.
Roadents—A squirrel that doesn't make it to the other side of the road.
Rolaids—Day-old donuts you feed your birds.
Round-Robin—An American thrush prior to hatching.
Rump Roast—A bird's posterior too close to the birdbath heater.
Rupture—A herniated hawk.

Sage—A wise bird singing in an arid bush.
Scrape—A shallow depression on the ground that serves as a bird's nest.

Shell-Shocked—The state of exhaustion most newborn birds experience after breaking out of the egg.

Shishkebobwhite—When a hawk takes a quail.

Shortfall—When a newborn killdeer falls out of his nest.

Shrub—An excellent woody plant for roosting and resting birds.

Slide Rule—Theory most birds use to determine approaching speed and braking distance prior to hitting the birdfeeder.

Species—A group of living things that look similar and can breed successfully.

Squirrel—Twenty pounds of walking sunflower seed; a rodent that has developed a habit of finding your birdseed before you know you've lost it.

Squirrel-Proof—An illusion that one has been successful in preventing a fur-bearing seed eater from ripping him off once again.

Stereoscenario—The belief that if you have seen one squirrel at your feeder, you're going to see them all.

Stoic—A boid what brings de babies.

Suetcide—The side of the birdfeeder you put the suet on.

Suicide—The use of insecticide and herbicide.

"Mom, I've got hare in my food!"

Talon—The quicker-picker-upper.

Territory—A bird's turf; a defended area with an imaginary perimeter that birds define with force.

Thermometer—A unique instrument to help you decide what to wear to the birdfeeder.

Thistlewhistle—The low clear musical sound made in disbelief when a bird finds fresh thistle seed in a birdfeeder.
Thrift—A frugal swift.
Triority—Feeding three baby birds at one time when the insects are not cooperating.

Vent—A birdseed exhaust pipe.
Virgin Forest—A wonderful bird habitat where the hand of man has never set foot.

Warehouse—What people say when they get lost going to the birdfeeder in a blinding snowstorm.
Wedge—How a bird places itself in a hedge when pursued by a sharp-shinned hawk.
Wigglemortis—A reaction that sets in when a worm knows he's been spotted by a robin.
Windowed—Losing a mate from a window strike.
Wing Bar—A popular neighborhood birdbath; a hummingbird feeder without a perch.
Winterize—Squinting at the feeder in a blizzard.
Wisecracks—Spaces in the eaves of a well-made birdhouse meant for ventilation.
Wrenagade—A free-thinking wren.

Yardschtick—Lame jokes you exchange with your neighbors while you're out filling your birdfeeder.
Yahoo—One who chases squirrels across the yard yelling like a cowboy on payday.
Yeeeeoooouucchh—The call of the cactus wren who sits down on the job.

Seasons of the Day

Every day begins a new season with dawn.
A subtle cycle unlike the explosion of spring,
Unlike the silence of fall. A collection,
Of tides and change, color and contrast.
Inherited habit, and raging senses.
Fields provide, marshes produce,
Woodlands gather sun and distribute shade.
Nothing moves that does not flow,
The new like the old, the fit precise.
Delicate but sturdy, intricate with ease.
Nature's marching arm in arm with time.

—Dick E. Bird